THE
ALL AMERICANS
IN
WORLD WAR II

A Photographic History of the
82nd Airborne Division at War

PHIL NORDYKE

ZENITH PRESS

This edition published by Zenith Press, an imprint of
MBI Publishing Company, Galtier Plaza, Suite 200,
380 Jackson Street, St. Paul, MN, 55101-3885 USA.

© Phil Nordyke, 2006

MBI Publishing Company Books are also available at discounts for
in bulk quantities for industrial or sale-promotional use. For details
write to Special Sales Manager at MBI Publishing Company,
Galtier Plaza, Suite 200, 380 Jackson Street,
St. Paul, MN, 55101-3885 USA

Cover by Tom Heffron
Layout by Brenda Canales
Maps by Phil Schwartzberg, Meridian Mapping

ISBN: 0-7603-2617-7
ISBN-13: 978-0-7603-2617-6

Printed in China

ON THE FRONT COVER:
Staff Sergeant James M. Martin of Cincinnati, Ohio, with Company F,
325th Glider Infantry Regiment, returning from outpost duty near
Ordimont, Belgium, during the Battle of the Bulge. *US Army photograph,
courtesy of the 82nd Airborne Division War Memorial Museum*

ON THE HALF-TITLE PAGE: General Gavin, with his parachute, reserve
chute, musette bag, and assembled M1 rifle, just before boarding his
plane, September 17, 1944. *U.S. Army photograph, courtesy of the 82nd
Airborne Division War Memorial Museum*

Contents

Chapter 1

"FIERCE INDIVIDUALISTS"

"There can be no such animal as a typical parachutist. Every 82nd Airborne trooper is by the nature of his mode of warfare an individualist of the first rank. His deeds individually and collectively are legend in the annals of American courage and initiative. His personality is as unpredictable as his dependability in combat."

—W. Forrest Dawson, *Saga of the All American*

Shortly after the Japanese attack on Pearl Harbor on December 7, 1944, young men from almost every background volunteered to join a new branch of the U.S. Army—the parachute forces. Private Ross S. Carter noted that "every level of society had its representation among us. Senators' sons rubbed shoulders with ex-cowboys. Steelworkers chummed up with tough guys from city slums. Farm boys, millionaires' spoiled brats, white-collar men, factory workers, ex-convicts, jailbirds, and hoboes joined for the thrill and adventure of parachute jumping. And so, the army's largest collection of adventurous men congregated in the parachute troops.

"The thing that distinguished us from most other soldiers was our willingness to take chances and risks in a branch of the army that provided a great, new, almost unexplored frontier. In other days paratroopers would have been the type to sail with Columbus, or the first to seek out the West and fight the Indians."

They underwent extremely tough physical training throughout the four weeks of jump school, during which many of the volunteers dropped out.

In February 1942, a division that had a legendary record for its actions in the First World War was reactivated—the 82nd Infantry Division. The greatest hero of that war had been Sergeant Alvin York, who had served with division and had been awarded the Congressional Medal of Honor. General Omar N. Bradley, the division commander, together with General Matthew B. Ridgway, the assistant division commander, instituted intensive physical training and instruction in weapons, tactics, and maneuver to build the division into a combat-ready force at Camp Claiborne, Louisiana.

The division's progress was so impressive that General Bradley was transferred to command the troubled 28th Infantry Division. On June 26, 1942, General Ridgway assumed command of the 82nd Division. On August 15, 1942, while completing the last weeks of training at Camp Claiborne, General Ridgway announced that the division would be converted into an airborne division and would provide the cadre for a second airborne division—the 101st. The infantry, artillery, antiaircraft, engineer, and headquarters units began training to become glider-borne.

On October 1, 1942, the 82nd Airborne Division was moved to Fort Bragg, North Carolina, where it was joined by the newly assigned 504th Parachute Infantry Regiment (PIR), the 376th Parachute Field Artillery (PFA) Battalion, and Company C, 307th Airborne Engineer Battalion. On February 12, 1943, due to a shortage of gliders, the 326th Glider Infantry Regiment (GIR) was transferred to the newly formed 13th Airborne Division, and the 505th Parachute Infantry Regiment, under the command of Colonel James M. Gavin, joined the 82nd Airborne Division.

A parachutist in training descends from one of the 250 towers at the jump school at Fort Benning. *U.S. Army photograph, courtesy of the 82nd Airborne Division War Memorial Museum*

A small portion of the tents and barracks at Camp Claiborne, Louisiana. *Photograph courtesy of www.campclaiborne.com*

Generals Bradley (left) and Ridgway use the rope swing to cross a water obstacle. *U.S. Army photograph, courtesy of the 82nd Airborne Division War Memorial Museum*

The 319th Field Artillery passes in review at Camp Claiborne. *U.S. Army photograph, courtesy of the 82nd Airborne Division War Memorial Museum*

Trainees at Fort Benning jump school perform left and right front tumbles in preparation for learning parachute landing falls (PLFs) during "B" Stage of jump school. *U.S. Army photograph*

The platform where trainees learn to execute PLFs. *U.S. Army photograph, courtesy of the 82nd Airborne Division War Memorial Museum*

Trainees practice exiting from a mockup of a C-47 door during "B" Stage. *U.S. Army photograph, courtesy of the 82nd Airborne Division War Memorial Museum*

Trainees practice using risers to guide the parachute. *U.S. Army photograph, courtesy of the 82nd Airborne Division War Memorial Museum*

Trainees practice handling and collapsing parachute canopies. *U.S. Army photograph, courtesy of the 82nd Airborne Division War Memorial Museum*

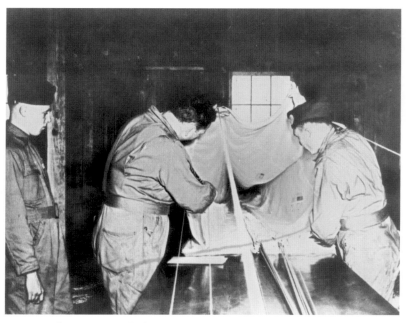

Trainees learn to pack their own parachutes on the last day of "C" Stage, for the qualifying jumps the following week. *U.S. Army photograph, courtesy of the 82nd Airborne Division War*

The dreaded thirty-four–foot tower during "C" Stage, where trainees exit from a mockup of a C-47 door and drop until their harness is caught by a cable, then guided to the ground. *U.S. Army photograph, courtesy of the 82nd Airborne Division War Memorial Museum*

Trainees line up with their parachutes on for an equipment check on the ground prior to a qualifying jump. Note the old football-type helmet worn by trainees at that time. *U.S. Army photograph*

The parachute is being pulled from the pack by a static line as the trainee falls. *U.S. Army photograph, courtesy of Weldon Grissom*

The parachute canopy begins to deploy as the trainee experiences the opening shock. *U.S. Army photograph, courtesy of Weldon Grissom*

After the parachute deploys, the trainee guides the chute to the ground. *U.S. Army photograph, courtesy of Weldon Grissom*

The trainee works to collapse his parachute canopy after landing. *U.S. Army photograph, courtesy of Weldon Grissom*

Chapter 2

"READY"

At Camp Mackall, the U.S. Army Airborne Command training facility near Fort Bragg, the intensity of the training increased during March and April of 1943, as secret preparations were underway to ship the division overseas. The glider-borne units used every available glider to practice loading, flying, and unloading equipment, artillery, antitank guns, jeeps, and troops. On March 30, 1943, the entire 505th Parachute Infantry Regiment executed the first mass parachute jump in U.S. Army history near Camden, South Carolina.

On April 17, 1943, the division began moving in strict secrecy by train from Fort Bragg to Camp Edwards, Massachusetts, in preparation for embarkation to its overseas destination. On April 29, the division departed New York City in a convoy of ships before dawn, landing at Casablanca, French Morocco, on May 10, 1943.

Two days later, the division moved over three hundred miles by train, truck, and air to Oujda, French Morocco. Their new encampment, which was located on a barren landscape, was made worse by swarms of locusts and flies, and a blazing sun. For the next six weeks, the paratroopers and glider troopers trained for an undisclosed mission. The heat was so intense that the division abandoned training during daylight hours in favor of night exercises, including live-fire assaults on trench and pillbox mock-ups constructed to simulate the objectives of the upcoming mission.

The division held a review for Generals George S. Patton, Mark Clark, and Omar Bradley on June 3, that included a daylight jump in full combat gear by the 3rd Battalion, 504th PIR, and the 3rd Battalion, 505th PIR. Winds exceeding thirty miles per hour caused many jump injuries.

On June 24, 1943, General Ridgway ordered the division to move to its staging areas, around Kairuoan, Tunisia to prepare for Operation Husky, the invasion of Sicily. A night combat jump during the early hours of July 10, 1943, by the 505th Regimental Combat Team (RCT) would spearhead the invasion. It consisted of the 505th Parachute Infantry Regiment; the 456th Parachute Field Artillery Battalion; Company B, 307th Airborne Engineer Battalion; and the 3rd Battalion, 504th Parachute Infantry Regiment. Colonel James M. Gavin, the commanding officer of the 505th Parachute Infantry Regiment, would command the regimental combat team. The 504th Regimental Combat Team, consisting of the 504th Parachute Infantry Regiment, less the 3rd Battalion; the 376th Parachute Field Artillery Battalion; and Company C, 307th Airborne Engineer Battalion, would make a night combat jump either the following night or the next, to reinforce Gavin's combat team. The 325th Regimental Combat Team and the 80th Airborne Antiaircraft (Antitank) Battalion would be held in reserve in Tunisia.

After all of the tough physical training, tactical maneuvers, planning, and rehearsals, General Ridgway had confidence in the 505th Regimental Combat Team and its commander: "By the takeoff time for Sicily, the men were so lean and tough, so mean and mad, that they would have jumped into the fires of torment just to get out of Africa. Gavin had done a prodigious job preparing for that attack, and we were ready, right down to the last round of ammunition."

Troopers charge from a CG-4A glider as part of a training exercise. *U.S. Army photograph, courtesy of the Silent Wings Museum*

Troopers congregate aboard one of the troop ships during the voyage from New York to Casablanca, French Morocco. *U.S. Army photograph, courtesy of the 82nd Airborne Division War Memorial Museum*

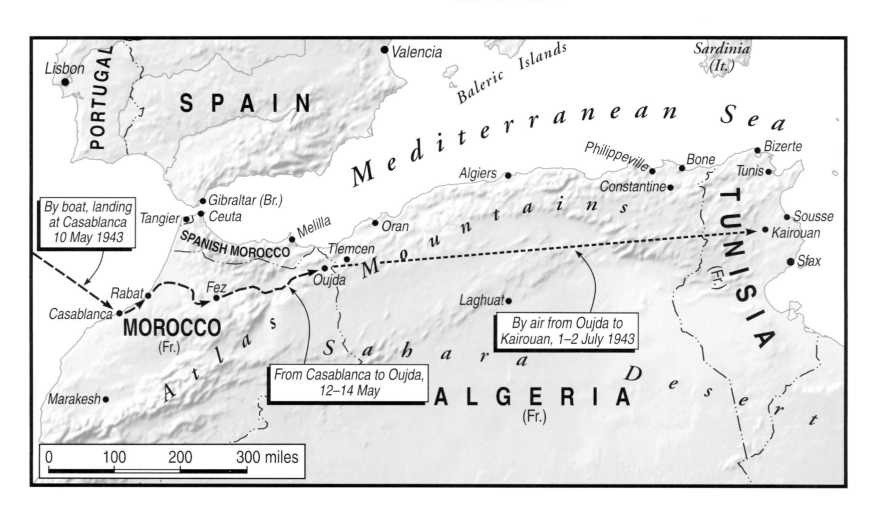

Aerial view of the encampment at Oujda, French Morocco. *U.S. Army photograph, courtesy of the 82nd Airborne Division War Memorial Museum*

Troopers practice hand-to-hand combat in gym shorts and jump boots during training in Oujda. *U.S. Army photograph, courtesy of the National Archives*

Paratroopers with Company E, 505th Parachute Infantry Regiment (PIR), leap from a platform to practice parachute landing falls. *U.S. Army photograph, courtesy of the National Archives*

A paratrooper is in the process of preparing an equipment bundle for the demonstration jump held at Oujda, June 3, 1943. *U.S. Army photograph, courtesy of the National Archives*

Colonel James M. Gavin, commander of the 505th PIR, and Major Benjamin H. Vandervoort, the S-3 operations officer, inspect troopers of the 3rd Battalion, 505th, prior to the demonstration jump on June 3, 1943. *U.S. Army photograph, courtesy of the 82nd Airborne Division War Memorial Museum*

Generals Mark Clark (front row, second from left), George S. Patton (front row, fourth from the left), Matthew B. Ridgway (front row, fifth from left), and Omar N. Bradley (front row, seventh from left), with foreign general officers and dignitaries, stand on the reviewing stand to watch the demonstration jump and parade by the 82nd Airborne Division. *U.S. Army photograph, courtesy of the 82nd Airborne Division War Memorial Museum*

Paratroopers from the 3rd Battalion, 504th PIR, and the 3rd Battalion, 505th PIR, descend over the drop zone near Oujda on June 3, 1943. *U.S. Army photograph, courtesy of the National Archives*

Paratroopers retrieve equipment bundle before moving to the assembly point, June 3, 1943. *U.S. Army photograph, courtesy of the National Archives*

Medical aid is given to a trooper injured during the demonstration jump in thirty plus mile per hour winds, June 3, 1943. *U.S. Army photograph, courtesy of the National Archives*

Colonel Gavin addresses paratroopers of the 505th PIR at the regiment's first-anniversary celebration and barbeque at Kairouan, Tunisia, July 6, 1943. *U.S. Army photograph, courtesy of the 82nd Airborne Division War Memorial Museum*

Glider troopers ride in a 40 & 8 boxcar from Oujda, French Morocco, to Kairouan, Tunisia. These boxcars were named for their ability to hold forty men or eight horses. *Photograph courtesy of Jan Bos*

Paratroopers of the 505th RCT load two equipment bundles onto the belly of their C-47 aircraft prior to takeoff to Sicily. *U.S. Army photograph, courtesy of the 82nd Airborne Division War Memorial Museum*

Chapter 3

"DESTROY HIM WHEREVER FOUND"

At 7:30 p.m. on July 9, 1943, 226 C-47 aircraft carrying the 505th RCT, with the 3rd Battalion, 504th attached began taking off for Sicily. This combat jump would spearhead the beach landings by the U.S. Seventh Army the next morning. A severe headwind encountered over the Mediterranean Sea near Malta broke up the formations of the five serials resulting in badly missed drops. What no one in the division knew was that the powerful Hermann Göring Panzer Division, with ninety Mark III and Mark IV tanks mounting 75mm main guns and seventeen Mark VI Tiger I tanks with the dreaded 88mm main guns, were positioned just miles north of their drop zone.

The 3rd Battalion, 504th PIR, in the first serial was badly scattered, but enough troopers landed near their drop zone to harass any enemy column moving south on the road from Niscemi to Gela, where the U.S. 1st Infantry Division would begin beach landings at 2:45 a.m. The road south from Niscemi, which ran through a narrow valley with hills on both sides, was the only route that afforded counterattacking enemy forces protection from U.S. naval gunfire. The crossroad where this road intersected the one running west from Vittoria was a natural chokepoint and was assigned to the entire 505th RCT as Objective "Y." The key crossroads were heavily fortified with pillboxes with mutually supporting fields of fire, trenches, minefields, and barbed wire.

The second serial into Sicily, the 3rd Battalion, 505th, commanded by Major Edward C. "Cannonball" Krause, was largely dropped far to the southeast of its drop zone, near Vittoria. Company I, 505th, had a separate mission, which was to seize another crossroads southeast of Objective "Y" on the highway from Vittoria to Gela. They were to light a fire on a hill to the east of Gela to act as a beacon to guide the predawn beach landings of the U.S. 1st Infantry Division. Company I, commanded by Captain Willard "Bill" Follmer, was the only company in the regiment to drop mostly on its drop zone, and then succeeded in carrying out its assignment.

The third serial, the 1st Battalion, 505th, commanded by Lieutenant Colonel Arthur "Hardnose" Gorham, was also scattered, except for the nine planes carrying part of battalion headquarters and Company A. The commanding officer of Company A, Captain Edwin Sayre, and about eighty troopers captured the regimental combat team's objective, the crossroads code-named "Y." They repulsed an armored attack later in the day and linked up with the U.S. 1st Infantry Division.

The regimental headquarters serial followed, with most of the sticks dropped south of Vittoria, far to the southeast of the drop zone. Colonel Gavin and a small group of his men worked their way toward Vittoria throughout the day, attempting to locate his regiment.

The last serial, the 2nd Battalion, 505th, commanded by Major Mark Alexander, was dropped about twenty-five miles southeast of the drop zone, but almost together, near Marina di Ragusa. The 2nd Battalion captured a series of pillboxes that it landed almost on top of, and then moved on to capture fortifications containing coastal artillery at Marina di Ragusa.

Troopers gather for an equipment check at the airfield near Kairouan, Tunisia, July 9, 1943. *U.S. Army photograph, courtesy of the 82nd Airborne Division War Memorial Museum*

Colonel Gavin just prior to boarding his aircraft for Sicily, July 9, 1943. *U.S. Army photograph, courtesy of the 82nd Airborne Division War Memorial Museum*

A paratrooper fastening the straps to his parachute harness and life preserver. *U.S. Army photograph, courtesy of the 82nd Airborne Division War Memorial Museum*

Paratroopers with the 505th RCT putting on their parachutes and equipment, July 9, 1943. *Photograph courtesy of Jan Bos*

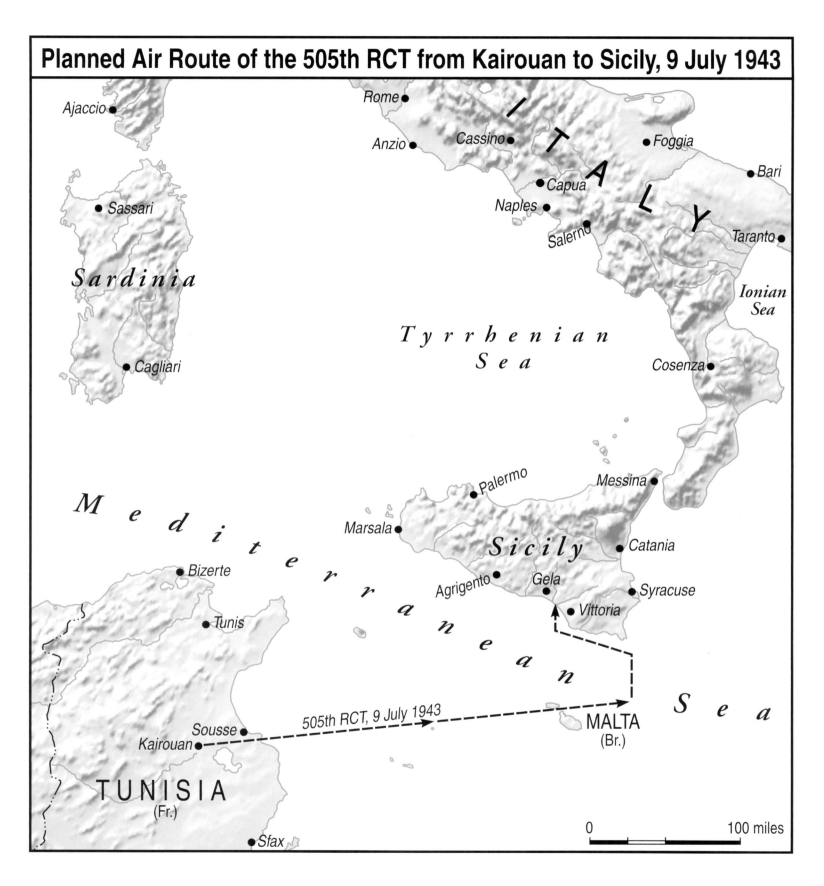

Planned Air Route of the 505th RCT from Kairouan to Sicily, 9 July 1943

Ajaccio

Rome

Cassino

Anzio

Foggia

ITALY

Bari

Capua

Naples

Sassari

Salerno

Taranto

Sardinia

Ionian Sea

Cagliari

T y r r h e n i a n
S e a

Cosenza

M e d i t e r r a

Palermo

Messina

Sicily

Marsala

Catania

Bizerte

Agrigento

Gela

Tunis

Syracuse

Vittoria

n e a n

S e a

505th RCT, 9 July 1943

MALTA
(Br.)

Sousse

Kairouan

TUNISIA
(Fr.)

0   100 miles

Sfax

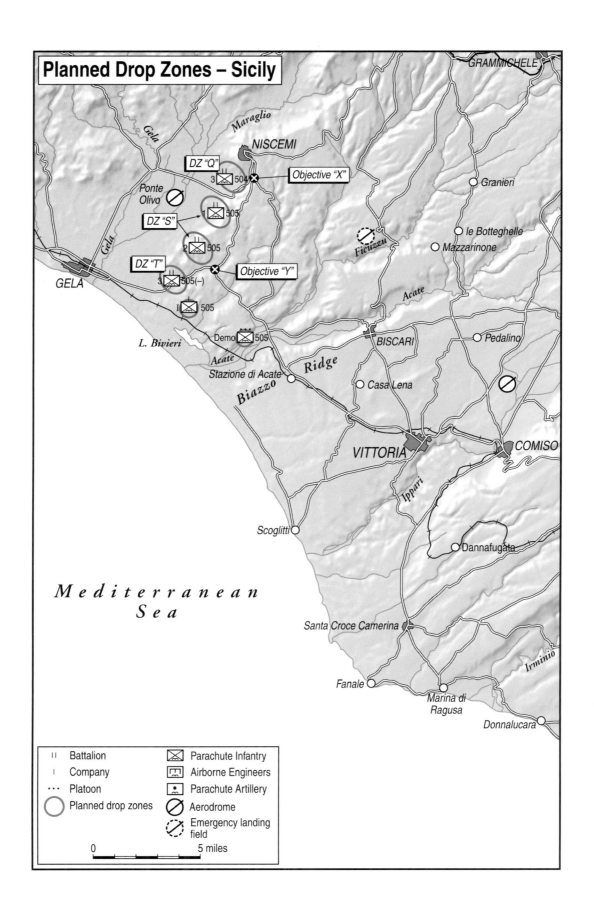

Planned Drop Zones – Sicily

GRAMMICHELE

Maraglio

Gela

NISCEMI

DZ "Q"

3 ⊠ 504 ⊗ Objective "X"

Ponte Olivo ⊘

1 ⊠ 505

DZ "S"

2 ⊠ 505

Gela

DZ "T"

Objective "Y"

GELA

3 ⊠ 505(−)

1 ⊠ 505

Demo ⊠ 505

L. Bivieri

Acate

Stazione di Acate ○

Biazzo Ridge

Acate

BISCARI

Granieri ○

Ficuzzu ⊘

le Botteghelle ○

Mazzarinone ○

Pedalino ○

Casa Lena ○

⊘

VITTORIA

COMISO

Ippari

Scoglitti ○

Dannafugata ○

Mediterranean Sea

Santa Croce Camerina ○

Fanale ○

Marina di Ragusa ○

Irminio

Donnalucara ○

‖ Battalion	⊠	Parachute Infantry
	Company	⊡	Airborne Engineers
⋯ Platoon	⊡	Parachute Artillery
○ Planned drop zones	⊘	Aerodrome
	⊘	Emergency landing field

0   5 miles

The 505th RCTs objective, code-named "Y," the key crossroads where the highways from Niscemi to the north and Vittoria to the east met northeast of Gela. Note the pillboxes just below the ridgeline in the upper right of the photograph. *U.S. Army photograph*

Stone and concrete pillbox in Sicily. *U.S. Army photograph, courtesy of the 82nd Airborne Division War Memorial Museum*

German Mark IV tank with 75mm long barreled main gun. *Author's collection*

German Mark VI Tiger I tank with 88mm high-velocity main gun. *Author's collection*

Chapter 4

"WE HAD A LONG WAY TO GO YET, AND SOME OF THE MEN WOULD ACCOMPANY US NO MORE"

On the morning of July 11, 1943, as Captain Ed Sayre and Lieutenant Colonel Arthur Gorham's 1st Battalion, 505th, paratroopers fought against the armored forces of the Western Kampfgruppe of the Hermann Göring Panzer Division, Colonel Gavin found the 3rd Battalion, 505th, just west of Vittoria. He immediately ordered Major Krause to get his battalion moving west on the highway to Gela.

Later that morning, as Gavin's force moved west toward Gela, it ran into the Eastern Kampfgruppe of the Hermann Göring Panzer Division, which included a company of seventeen Mark VI Tiger tanks at a slight ridge, forever after known as Biazzo Ridge. Gavin's lightly armed paratroopers drove the German infantry off of the ridge and moved down the reverse slope, only to encounter several Tiger tanks as well as machine gun and mortar fire. The troopers were heavily outgunned, and their bazookas were practically useless against the German armor. The Germans counterattacked and threatened to retake the ridge. Finally, aided by naval gunfire and artillery from the U.S. 45th Division, Gavin's men succeeded in driving off the German force after an all-day fight.

That night, the 504th RCT, less the 3rd Battalion, took off from Tunisia in 144 C-47 aircraft to land by parachute in Sicily to reinforce Gavin's combat team. As the aircraft carrying Colonel Rueben Tucker's force arrived over the coast of Sicily in the wake of a German air raid on the fleet of warships offshore, they were mistaken for enemy aircraft and were fired upon by the naval ships and the 45th Division antiaircraft guns. Twenty-three planes were shot down and another thirty-seven were damaged. The 504th RCT lost 81 killed, 16 missing, and 132 wounded from the disastrous friendly fire.

For the next week, a consolidation and reorganization of the two regimental combat teams took place along with the arrival of 426 officers and men by daylight glider landing. On July 20, 1943, Ridgway's force began advancing up Highway 115, which paralleled the Sicilian coast, to the town of Trapani, on the northwestern tip of the island. The troopers met spotty resistance by mostly Italian forces, all too ready to surrender. After capturing Trapani on July 23, the troopers settled into performing occupation duties.

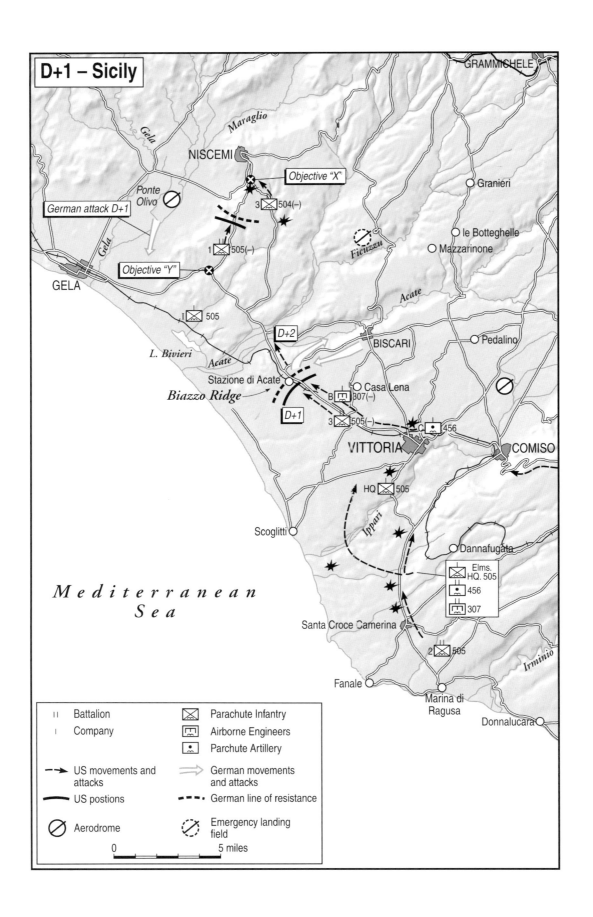

D+1 – Sicily

GRAMMICHELE

Maraglio

Gela

NISCEMI

Objective "X"

3 ⊠ 504(–)

German attack D+1

Ponte Olivo

1 ⊠ 505(–)

Ficuzzu

○ Granieri

○ le Botteghelle

○ Mazzarinone

Gela

Objective "Y"

GELA

1 ⊠ 505

Acate

○ Pedalino

L. Bivieri

Acate

D+2

BISCARI

Stazione di Acate

Biazzo Ridge

○ Casa Lena

B ⊡ 307(–)

D+1

3 ⊠ 505(–)

C ⊡ 456

COMISO

VITTORIA

HQ ⊠ 505

○ Scoglitti

Ippari

○ Dannafugata

M e d i t e r r a n e a n
S e a

⊠ Elms. HQ. 505

⊡ 456

⊡ 307

Santa Croce Camerina

2 ⊠ 505

Irminio

○ Fanale

Marina di Ragusa

○ Donnalucara

‖	Battalion	⊠ Parachute Infantry
ǀ	Company	⊡ Airborne Engineers
		⊡ Parchute Artillery

- - -► US movements and attacks
⟹ German movements and attacks

━━ US postions
– – – German line of resistance

⊘ Aerodrome
⊘ Emergency landing field

0   5 miles

Troopers of the 3rd Battalion, 505th PIR advance to the top of Biazzo Ridge, July 11, 1943. *U.S. Army photograph, courtesy of the 82nd Airborne Division War Memorial Museum*

An 81mm mortar is set up on the east side of Biazzo Ridge to provide supporting fire for paratroopers of the 3rd Battalion, 505th PIR. *U.S. Army photograph, courtesy of the 82nd Airborne Division War Memorial Museum*

The first Tiger tank captured by the 82nd Airborne Division, on the side of the Vittoria-Gela highway on the west side of Biazzo Ridge. *U.S. Army photograph, courtesy of the 82nd Airborne Division War Memorial Museum*

Lieutenant Harold H. "Swede" Swingler, with Regimental Headquarters Company, 505th, single-handedly killed the crew of the same Mark VI Tiger tank pictured in the previous photo with a hand grenade. *U.S. Army photograph, courtesy of the 82nd Airborne Division War Memorial Museum*

Major Edward "Cannonball" Krause, the commander of the 3rd Battalion, 505th PIR, poses next to a German 75mm antitank gun captured west of Biazzo Ridge, July 11, 1943. *U.S. Army photograph, courtesy of the 82nd Airborne Division War Memorial Museum*

German POWs, former members of the Hermann Göring Division captured the previous day, dig graves for troopers of the 505th killed during the Battle of Biazzo Ridge, July12, 1943. *U.S. Army photograph, courtesy of Jerome V. Huth*

Colonel Rueben H. Tucker, holding a folding stock carbine, prepares to board his C-47 for the flight to Sicily, July 11, 1943. *U.S. Army photograph, courtesy of the 82nd Airborne Division War Memorial Museum*

Captain Adam A. Komosa's stick of Company D, 504th PIR, paratroopers prior to takeoff for Sicily. *Adam A. Komosa photograph, courtesy of the 82nd Airborne Division War Memorial Museum*

The few troopers of the 82nd Airborne Division who have motor transport, move through the town of Sciacca, Sicily, July 20, 1943. *U.S. Army photograph, courtesy of the 82nd Airborne Division War Memorial Museum*

Others ride captured weapons carriers, buses, motorcycles, trucks, and donkey carts. *U.S. Army photograph, courtesy of the 82nd Airborne Division War Memorial Museum*

Paratroopers ride captured Italian tankettes during the advance to Trapani, Sicily. *U.S. Army photograph, courtesy of the 82nd Airborne Division War Memorial Museum*

Locals of one of the Sicilian towns in the 82nd Airborne Division's line of advance turn out to watch the troopers of the division as they wait for traffic ahead to clear. *U.S. Army photograph, courtesy of the 82nd Airborne Division War Memorial Museum*

Troopers line up for ice cream at a small town during their advance to Trapani. *U.S. Army photograph, courtesy of the 82nd Airborne Division War Memorial Museum*

Three troopers enjoy eating ice cream during a break in their advance to Trapani. *U.S. Army photograph, courtesy of the 82nd Airborne Division War Memorial Museum*

After their break, troopers move out, crossing railroad tracks as they advance toward Trapani. *U.S. Army photograph, courtesy of the 82nd Airborne Division War Memorial Museum*

Chapter 5

"RETREAT HELL!— SEND ME MY 3RD BATTALION!"

After the Sicily campaign, the division set up a pathfinder school at Comiso, Sicily, to develop techniques to guide troop-carrier aircraft to the drop zones more accurately. Handpicked paratroopers from the 504th and 505th were trained in the use of electronic beacons and direction finding devices, together with lights to mark the drop zones. After training, tests using the Eureka transponder to guide pathfinder C-47 aircraft equipped with the Rebecca transmitter proved successful, as did tests of Aldis lamps and Krypton lights to illuminate drop zones.

After a planned jump northwest of Naples in support of American and British landings on the Italian mainland in the Bay of Salerno, and another near Rome were cancelled, the division was at airfields in Sicily on September 13, when General Ridgway received an urgent note from General Mark Clark. Strong German armored forces had launched a fierce counterattack on the Salerno beachhead and were threatening to drive down to the beach in the American sector. General Clark's note requested a parachute drop that night on the beach inside of American lines, to prevent his force from having to evacuate.

Eight hours later, planes carrying Tucker's 1st and 2nd Battalions of the 504th PIR and Company C, 307th Airborne Engineer Battalion, began lifting off. Pathfinders from the 504th using Eurekas and flaming fifty-five gallon oil drums guided the aircraft to the drop zone, and Tucker's paratroopers were dropped on the beach shortly before midnight. After assembling, the 504th moved up to plug the gap in the American line. The following night the 505th PIR and Company B, 307th Airborne Engineer Battalion, made the same drop, using 505th pathfinders to guide the planes to the drop zone.

On the afternoon of September 16, the two battalions of the 504th began an infiltration attack to recapture three key hills southeast of Altavilla. After marching through the night, the two battalions were in possession of those hills by dawn. Throughout September 17, Tucker's men endured heavy shelling and threw back assault after assault by German infantry. That night, the corps commander told Tucker over a sound powered phone that the 504th was surrounded and should withdraw to prevent the same fate that a battalion of the 36th Division had suffered earlier on those same hills. Tucker's reply was, "Retreat Hell!— Send me my 3rd Battalion!"

Tucker's troopers held that night, and patrols the next morning revealed that the Germans had withdrawn. The beachhead at Salerno was saved.

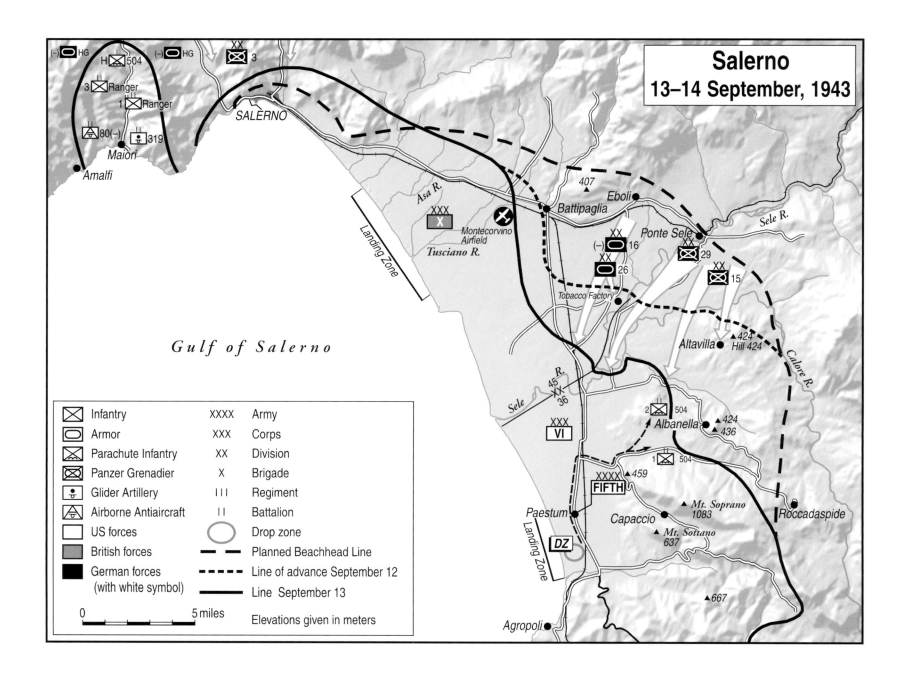

Salerno
13–14 September, 1943

(–) HG   HG   XX 3

H 504

3 Ranger

1 Ranger

SALERNO

80(–)   319

Maiori

Amalfi

Asa R.

407

Eboli

XXX X   *Battipaglia*

Montecorvino Airfield

Tusciano R.

Ponte Sele

(–) 16   XX 29

26   XX 15

Sele R.

Tobacco Factory

Gulf of Salerno

424 Hill 424

Altavilla

Calore R.

Sele R.

XX 36

45

XXX VI

2 504

Albanella   424   436

1 504

XXXX FIFTH   459

Paestum

Capaccio

Mt. Soprano 1083

Roccadaspide

DZ

Mt. Sottano 637

667

Agropoli

Legend

Symbol	Description	Symbol	Description
Infantry	XXXX	Army
Armor	XXX	Corps
Parachute Infantry	XX	Division
Panzer Grenadier	X	Brigade
Glider Artillery	III	Regiment
Airborne Antiaircraft	II	Battalion
US forces	⬭	Drop zone
British forces	— — —	Planned Beachhead Line
German forces (with white symbol)	·········	Line of advance September 12
	⸺⸺	Line September 13

0   5 miles

Elevations given in meters

The camp at Trapani, set up by the 82nd Airborne Division to hold Italian POWs. *Photograph courtesy of Mrs. Ann McIlvoy Zaya*

Paratroopers with the 505th RCT land at Tripoli, Libya, after being dropped in the British zone in Sicily and evacuated by the British navy. *U.S. Army photograph, courtesy of the 82nd Airborne Division War Memorial Museum*

C-47s on the taxiway of an airfield in Sicily, ready for takeoff to Italy. *U.S. Army photograph, courtesy of the 82nd Airborne Division War Memorial Museum*

A pathfinder with a leg bag containing a Eureka homing device, used by pathfinders to guide aircraft to the drop zone at Paestum, Italy. *Photograph courtesy of Jerome V. Huth*

"WAIT UNTIL A TRIUMPHANT ENTRY IS ORGANIZED"

On the left flank of the Salerno beachhead, Company H, 504th PIR, as part of a seaborne force from the 82nd Airborne Division that included the 319th Glider Field Artillery Battalion and Batteries D, E, and F, 80th Airborne Antiaircraft (Antitank) Battalion, which landed on September 10, had been holding the critical Chiunzi Pass against almost daily attacks by the Germans. Water, rations, and ammunition, which had to be hauled up the mountains on foot or in a few cases by mule, were always in short supply.

Companies E and F, 325th Glider Infantry Regiment, relieved U.S. Army Rangers on Mt. San Angelo and Mt. di Chiunzi on September 18. The next morning, a large German force hit Company E, 325th on Mt. San Angelo, overrunning one of its squad positions, before a counterattack restored the position.

That day, the 504th PIR, less Company H, and the 325th GIR, less the 2nd Battalion, were relieved. On September 20 they were sent by landing craft to Maiori, where the 504th moved up to relieve Company H, which had held the Chiunzi Pass for ten days. On September 25, Company B, 325th GIR, relieved Company E, while Company A attacked and destroyed a German force dug in on the northern slope of Mt. San Angelo. The division's seaborne force was later awarded the division's first Distinguished Unit Citation for its actions.

On September 27 and 28, the 505th PIR, led by the 3rd Battalion, pushed through the Chiunzi Pass and then across the plains south of Naples against rear-guard enemy forces, advancing to the outskirts of the city by October 1, 1943. Colonel Gavin was up front with the lead elements of the 3rd Battalion, "when the Regimental S-3, Major Jack Norton approached.

"'Colonel,' he said. 'We are to wait until a triumphant entry is organized.'

"'A triumphant entry!' I exclaimed."

General Mark Clark had ordered the "triumphant entry" so that the newsreel cameras and press could see him entering Naples at the head of a conquering army. However, because of the danger faced in entering an unsecured city, General Ridgway sent word to the Naples police chief to clear the streets, and the entry was made into Naples with mostly empty streets.

The division occupied Naples for the next month and a half. From October 4 to 7, the 1st and 2nd Battalions, 505th, were attached to the British 22nd Armoured Brigade to capture five canal bridges near the Volturno River. The 504th RCT was attached to the U.S. 34th Infantry Division on October 27, and fought in the Apennine Mountains and along the valley of the Volturno River, capturing Hill 1017 in hard fighting.

Colonel James Gavin was promoted to brigadier general and assistant division commander in early November of 1943. Colonel Herbert Batcheller replaced Gavin as commander of the 505th PIR.

On November 18, the division sailed from Naples to Northern Ireland to prepare for the invasion of northwest Europe, while the 504th RCT was reluctantly left behind to fight in Italy, at the insistence of General Mark Clark.

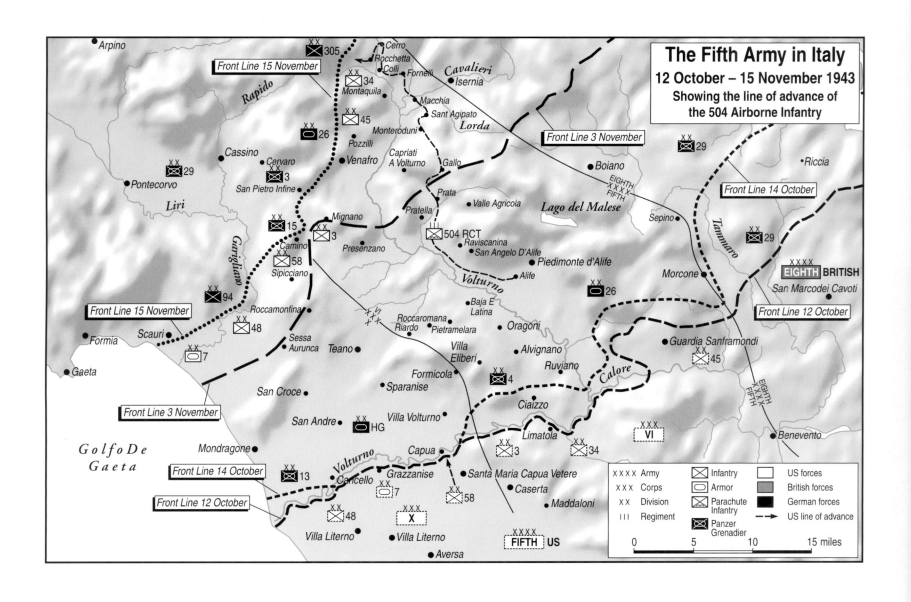

The Fifth Army in Italy
12 October – 15 November 1943
Showing the line of advance of
the 504 Airborne Infantry

Arpino

Front Line 15 November

Cerro
Rocchetta
Colli
Fornelli
Cavalieri
Isernia

305

34
Montaquila

Rapido

45

26

Pozzilli

Macchia
Sant Agipato
Lorda

Front Line 3 November

29

Riccia

Cassino
Cervaro
3
San Pietro Infine

Venafro

Monteroduni

Capriati
A Volturno
Gallo

Boiano

EIGHTH
XXXX
FIFTH

Sepino

29

Tammaro

Front Line 14 October

Pontecorvo

29

Prata

Liri

Pratella

Valle Agricola

Lago del Malese

15
Mignano

3

Camino

58

Sipicciano

Presenzano

504 RCT

Raviscanina
San Angelo D'Alife

Piedimonte d'Alife

Volturno

Alife

29

Morcone

San Marcodei Cavoti

EIGHTH
XXXX
FIFTH

Front Line 12 October

Gargliano

Roccamonfina

94

Baja E
Latina

26

Front Line 15 November

Scauri

48

Roccaromana
Riardo
Pietramelara

Oragoni

Guardia Sanframondi

Formia

7

Sessa
Aurunca

Teano

Villa
Eliberi

Alvignano

Ruviano

45

Gaeta

Calore

Front Line 3 November

San Croce

Formicola

Sparanise

Ciaizzo

Benevento

Villa Volturno

San Andre

HG

Golfo De
Gaeta

Mondragone

Volturno

Capua

Limatola

VI

Front Line 14 October

13

Cancello
Grazzanise

7

Santa Maria Capua Vetere

Caserta

3

34

Front Line 12 October

58

Maddaloni

X

48
Villa Literno
Villa Literno

FIFTH US

Aversa

XXXX Army	Infantry	US forces
XXX Corps	Armor	British forces
XX Division	Parachute Infantry	German forces
III Regiment	Panzer Grenadier	US line of advance

0   5   10   15 miles

General Mark Clark expresses his appreciation to troopers of the 325th Glider Infantry Regiment (GIR) for their actions on Mt. di Chiunzi and Mt. San Angelo. *U.S. Army photograph, courtesy of the 82nd Airborne Division War Memorial Museum*

Engineers with the 307th Airborne Engineer Battalion repair a bridge blown by the Germans in the Sorrento Mountains during their retreat north to Naples. *U.S. Army photograph, courtesy of the 82nd Airborne Division War Memorial Museum*

Paratroopers with Headquarters Company, 2nd Battalion, 505th PIR, enter Naples, October 2, 1943. *U.S. Army photograph, courtesy of the National Archives*

Private Dickie Hensley, of Mexia, Texas, holds a little girl, one of eight civilians killed when Germans blew up a roadblock in the town of Prata, Italy, November 1, 1943. *U.S. Army photograph, courtesy of the National Archives*

Members of the 504th RCT move through a devastated village during their advance through the Apennine Mountains. *U.S. Army photograph, courtesy of the 82nd Airborne Division War Memorial Museum*

A trooper with Company C, 307th Airborne Engineer Battalion, leads the way using a metal detector to sweep for German landmines, as the 504th RCT advances in the Apennine Mountains. *U.S. Army photograph, courtesy of the 82nd Airborne Division War Memorial Museum*

A 75mm pack howitzer of the 376th Parachute Field Artillery Battalion fires in support of the infantry in the Apennine Mountains. *U.S. Army photograph, courtesy of the 82nd Airborne Division War Memorial Museum*

Troopers lay communication wire in the mountains, working to maintain communications between the 376th Parachute Field Artillery Battalion and the 504th PIR, fighting in the mountains above. This was always dangerous work because of landmines and enemy snipers. *U.S. Army photograph, courtesy of the 82nd Airborne Division War Memorial Museum*

Personnel with the 307th Medical Company attached to the 504th RCT and ambulance drivers with Service Company, 504th, carefully remove patients from an ambulance. Both of these units performed heroically to save as many lives as possible during the fighting in the Apennine Mountains. *U.S. Army photograph, courtesy of the 82nd Airborne Division War Memorial Museum*

Radio operators from all units of the 504th RCT worked hard to maintain contact despite difficulties with radio signal reception in the mountainous terrain. *U.S. Army photograph*

Troopers with the 504th PIR share K-rations after a long and difficult day in the mountains. *U.S. Army photograph, courtesy of the 82nd Airborne Division War Memorial Museum*

The view of Mount Sammucro, known as Hill 1205 to the paratroopers of the 504th RCT. *Photograph courtesy of James Megellas*

Lieutenant James Megellas and Sergeant Michael Kogut, both with Company H, 504th PIR, clean their weapons on Hill 610, known as the "the Pimple." *Photograph courtesy of James Megellas*

These two mules are hauling 81mm mortars for troopers of the 504th PIR. Mules were used wherever available to carry water, rations, ammunition, and crew-served weapons. *U.S. Army photograph, courtesy of the 82nd Airborne Division War Memorial Museum*

A trooper takes a .30-caliber machine gun hauled by a mule in the Apennine Mountains. *U.S. Army photograph, courtesy of the 82nd Airborne Division War Memorial Museum*

Two troopers with the 504th PIR fire a .30-caliber machine gun from an opening in a rocky ledge, December 18, 1943. *U.S. Army photograph, courtesy of the National Archives via Martin K. A. Morgan*

Chapter 7

"DEVILS IN BAGGY PANTS"

On December 9, 1943, the same day that the 82nd Airborne Division arrived in Northern Ireland, the 504th RCT moved to Venafro, Italy. Two days later, the 3rd Battalion, 504th relieved the 3rd Ranger Battalion on Hill 950, while the 2nd Battalion, 504th reinforced the 1st Battalion, 143rd Infantry on Mt. Sammucro (Hill 1205), and the 1st Battalion, 504th was held in reserve on Mt. Sammucro. The fighting was vicious, with the hills and areas leading to them heavily mined, contributing to high casualties. Enemy snipers were a constant problem, and artillery barrages added to the losses.

Between December 14 and 18, the 504th captured Hills 954 and 687 as part of the effort by the U.S. 36th Infantry Division to put pressure on the German forces holding the town of San Pietro. The 504th RCT was relieved on December 27, with attrition having reduced most of the rifle companies to around twenty to thirty officers and men per company.

The authorized infantry strength of the 82nd Airborne Division was temporarily increased to four regiments for the upcoming invasion of northwest Europe. Because the 504th RCT was still in Italy, the untested 507th PIR and the 508th PIR, fresh from training in the United States, were attached to the division on January 20, 1944.

Two days later, the 504th RCT waded ashore after the U.S. 3rd Infantry Division at Anzio, Italy. The regimental combat team captured two vital bridges across the Mussolini Canal as part of the assignment to protect the southern flank of the beachhead. The 504th RCT, except for the 3rd Battalion, spent most of the next month fighting along the area on both sides of the Mussolini Canal.

The 3rd Battalion, 504th, was assigned to the British 24th Brigade on February 1, on the northern side of the beachhead. On the night of February 3–4, the Germans broke through the British lines and moved south, threatening to drive all the way to the beach. The severely depleted 3rd Battalion, 504th, moved in to plug the gap and stopped the German penetration in its tracks, earning a Distinguished Unit Citation.

The reputation of the 504th RCT paratroopers grew as they met the Germans in numerous engagements and night patrols. A diary found on the body of a dead German officer read, "American parachutists—devils in baggy pants—are less than one hundred meters from my outpost line. I can't sleep at night. They pop up from nowhere and we never know when or how they will strike next. Seems the black-hearted devils are everywhere."

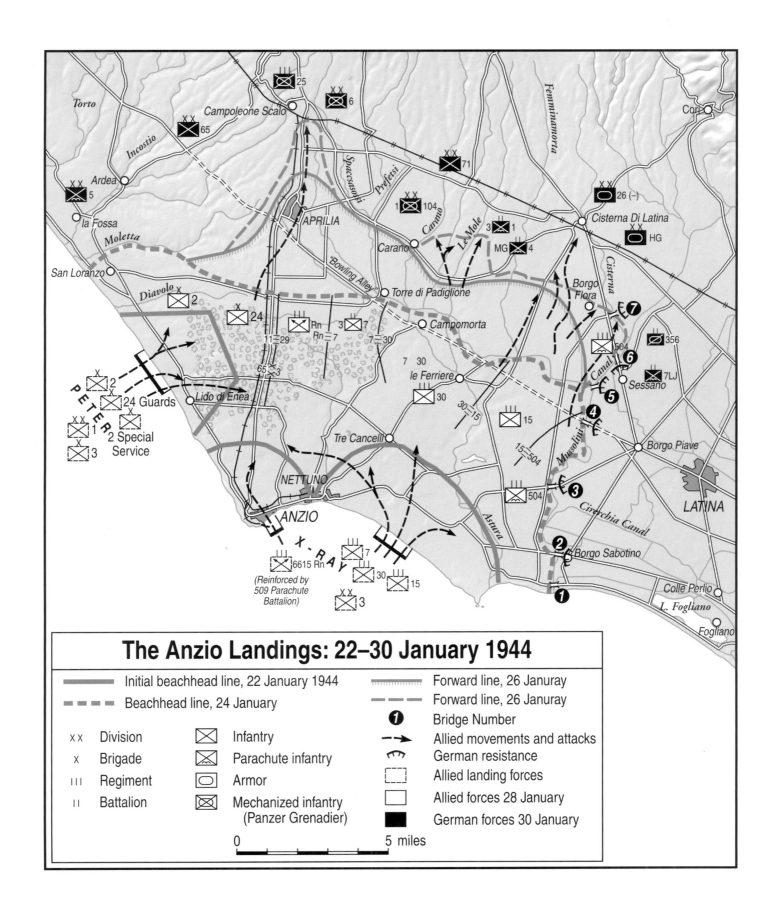

The Anzio Landings: 22–30 January 1944

Map labels:

Torto · *Incostio* · Campoleone Scalo · 25 · 6 · 65 · *Femminamorta* · Cori
Ardea · 5 · *Carano* · *Prefetsi* · *Spaccsasossi* · 71 · 26 (–) · *Cisterna Di Latina* · HG
la Fossa · APRILIA · 104 · 3 · 1 · *Le Mole* · *Cisterna*
Moletta · Carano · MG · 4 · *Borgo Flora* · 7
San Loranzo · *Diavolo* · 2 · 24 · Torre di Padiglione · 356 · 504 · 6
11─29 · Rn─7 · 3 · 7 · Campomorta · *Canal* · 5 · 7LJ · *Sessano*
Rn · 7─30 · 7 · 30 · le Ferriere · 30 · 30─15 · 4
65─3 · 30 · 15 · 15─504 · *Musolini* · Borgo Piave
P E T E R · 2 · 24 Guards · Lido di Enea · Tre Cancelli · 15─504 · 3
1 · 2 Special Service · 3 · NETTUNO · 504 · LATINA
X · R A Y · ANZIO · 2 · Borgo Sabotino
6615 Rn · 7 · 1 · Colle Perlio
(Reinforced by 509 Parachute Battalion) · 30 · 15 · 3 · *L. Fogliano*
Fogliano

Legend

Symbol	Meaning	Symbol	Meaning
▬▬▬	Initial beachhead line, 22 January 1944	⊥⊥⊥⊥⊥	Forward line, 26 Januray
▪▪▪▪	Beachhead line, 24 January	▬ ▬ ▬	Forward line, 26 Januray
x x	Division	❶	Bridge Number
x	Brigade	→→	Allied movements and attacks
|||	Regiment	⌒	German resistance
||	Battalion	⬚	Allied landing forces
⊠	Infantry	☐	Allied forces 28 January
⊠	Parachute infantry	■	German forces 30 January
⬭	Armor		
⊠	Mechanized infantry (Panzer Grenadier)		

0   5 miles

Troopers of the 82nd Airborne Division are crowded on the deck of their ship during the voyage to Northern Ireland. *U.S. Army photograph, courtesy of the 82nd Airborne Division War Memorial Museum*

With their rifles slung, 504th PIR troopers, follow mules heavily laden with crew-served weapons, ammunition, and rations up a mountain path near Venafro, Italy, December 12, 1943. *U.S. Army photograph, courtesy of the National Archives*

These six troopers share a small stateroom on their ship during the journey to Northern Ireland. *U.S. Army photograph, courtesy of the 82nd Airborne Division War Memorial Museum*

Paratroopers with the 504th PIR move along a mountain road past a knocked-out Sherman tank near San Pietro, Italy, December 17, 1943. *U.S. Army photograph courtesy of the National Archives*

Troopers with the 504th PIR wade ashore on the Anzio beachhead. *U.S. Army photograph, courtesy of the 82nd Airborne Division War Memorial Museum*

Troopers wait in a ditch as tanks move forward during the attack toward Cisterna, Italy, January 26, 1944. *U.S. Army photograph, courtesy of the 82nd Airborne Division War Memorial Museum*

An 81mm mortar crew and a mule pressed into service, set up on the bank of the Mussolini Canal. *U.S. Army photograph, courtesy of the 82nd Airborne Division War Memorial Museum*

Wounded troopers from the 504th RCT are evacuated from the Anzio beachhead. *U.S. Army photograph, courtesy of the 82nd Airborne Division War Memorial Museum*

The 2nd Battalion, 504th crosses the Mussolini Canal during the attack toward Cisterna, Italy, January 26, 1944. *U.S. Army photograph, courtesy of the 82nd Airborne Division War Memorial Museum*

Chapter 8

"YOU ARE ABOUT TO EMBARK UPON THE GREAT CRUSADE"

The 82nd Airborne Division began moving from Northern Ireland to bases in the Leicester and Nottingham areas of England, beginning on February 13, 1944. Intense training began immediately to prepare the division for its missions in the upcoming invasion of northwest Europe.

Because of disciplinary problems with the 505th PIR, Colonel Batcheller was relieved and replaced as commander by Lieutenant Colonel William E. Ekman, the executive officer of the 508th PIR, who took command of the 505th PIR on March 22.

After sixty-one days in combat, the 504th RCT was relieved at the Anzio beachhead and left for Naples. After a few weeks of rest, the 504th RCT sailed for England, arriving on April 22. The regimental combat team was so badly depleted from the fighting at Anzio that General Ridgway made the decision to leave it out of the upcoming jump, and hold it in reserve in England instead.

The initial plan for which the division prepared was for a jump near St.-Sauveur-le-Vicomte on the Cotentin Peninsula of Normandy, France, although the location was top secret and not divulged to anyone in the division without the proper security clearance and a need to know. Security was very tight around the regimental and division command headquarters as map overlays, sand tables, and mission plans were being drawn up.

In late May, the discovery by aerial photo reconnaissance of the presence of elements of the German 91st Airlanding Division around St.-Sauveur-le-Vicomte caused planners to scrap the plan for which

every unit in the division had been trained. A new plan was quickly formulated for capturing the key crossroads town of Ste.-Mère-Église and the causeways across the Merderet River to prevent German counterattacks on the landings at Utah Beach. The division moved to airfields at the end of May, and after being sealed in, all units were briefed about the new plan and their individual unit missions.

On the evening of June 5, 1944, every man in the division received a note from General Eisenhower:

> SOLDIERS, SAILORS, AND AIRMEN OF THE ALLIED EXPEDITIONARY FORCE!
>
> YOU ARE ABOUT TO EMBARK UPON THE GREAT CRUSADE, TOWARD WHICH WE HAVE STRIVEN THESE MANY MONTHS. THE EYES OF THE WORLD ARE UPON YOU. THE HOPES AND PRAYERS OF LIBERTY-LOVING PEOPLE EVERYWHERE MARCH WITH YOU. IN COMPANY WITH OUR BRAVE ALLIES AND BROTHERS-IN-ARMS ON OTHER FRONTS, YOU WILL BRING ABOUT THE DESTRUCTION OF THE GERMAN WAR MACHINE, THE ELIMINATION OF NAZI TYRANNY OVER THE OPPRESSED PEOPLES OF EUROPE, AND SECURITY FOR OURSELVES IN A FREE WORLD . . . .

At about 10:30 p.m. the first nine planes carrying the division pathfinders began lifting off from their airfield, heading for Normandy.

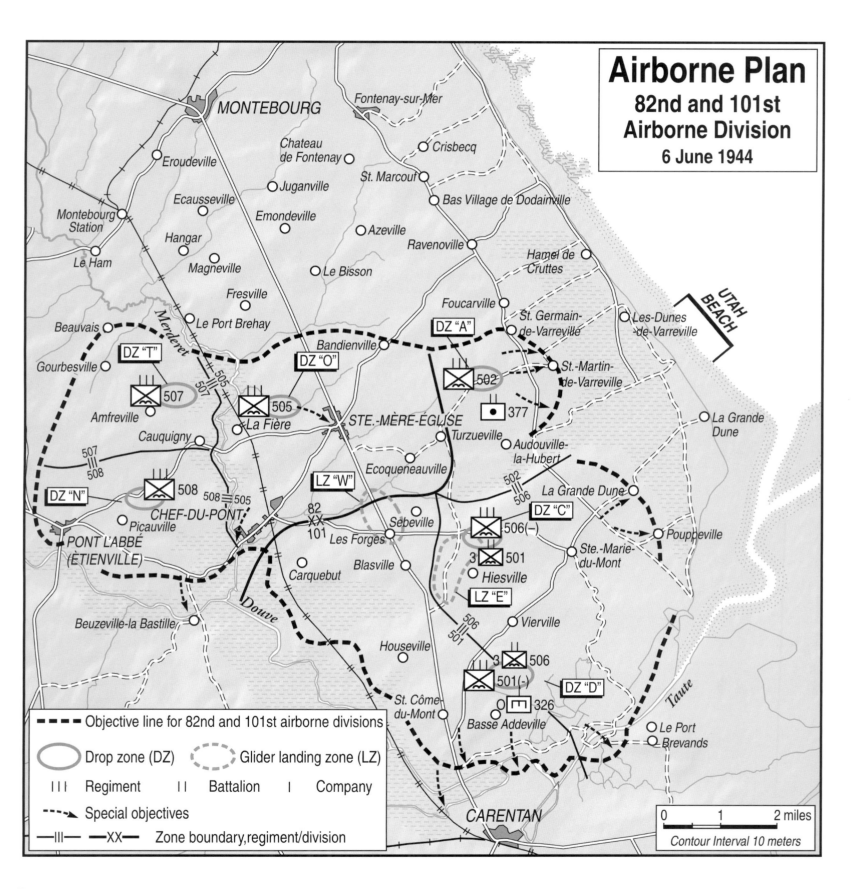

Airborne Plan
82nd and 101st Airborne Division
6 June 1944

MONTEBOURG
Fontenay-sur-Mer
Chateau de Fontenay
Crisbecq
Eroudeville
St. Marcouf
Juganville
Ecausseville
Bas Village de Dodainville
Montebourg Station
Emondeville
Azeville
Ravenoville
Hamel de Cruttes
Hangar
Le Bisson
UTAH BEACH
Le Ham
Magneville
Foucarville
St. Germain-de-Varreville
Les-Dunes-de-Varreville
Fresville
DZ "A"
Beauvais
Merderet
Le Port Brehay
Bandienville
DZ "T"
DZ "O"
St.-Martin-de-Varreville
502
Gourbesville
507
505
507
505
505
La Grande Dune
507 508
La Fière
STE.-MÈRE-ÉGLISE
377
Amfreville
Turzueville
Audouville-la-Hubert
Cauquigny
507 508
Ecoqueneauville
508
LZ "W"
502 506
La Grande Dune
DZ "N"
508
505
CHEF-DU-PONT
82 XX 101
Sebeville
DZ "C"
Picauville
Les Forges
506(-)
Pouppeville
PONT L'ABBÉ (ÉTIENVILLE)
3 501
Ste.-Marie-du-Mont
Blasville
Hiesville
Carquebut
LZ "E"
Beuzeville-la-Bastille
Douve
Houseville
Vierville
506 501
3 506
501(-)
DZ "D"
Taute
326
St. Côme-du-Mont
Basse Addeville
Le Port
Brevands

Legend:
- - - Objective line for 82nd and 101st airborne divisions
⬭ Drop zone (DZ) ⬭ Glider landing zone (LZ)
||| Regiment || Battalion | Company
--→ Special objectives
—|||— —XX— Zone boundary, regiment/division

CARENTAN

0   1   2 miles
Contour Interval 10 meters

42

The 2nd Battalion, 505th PIR tents at Camp Quorn, March 1944. *Photograph courtesy of the 82nd Airborne Division War Memorial Museum*

Waco CG-4A gliders being assembled for use in the invasion of northwest Europe. *U.S. Army photograph, courtesy of the 82nd Airborne Division War Memorial Museum*

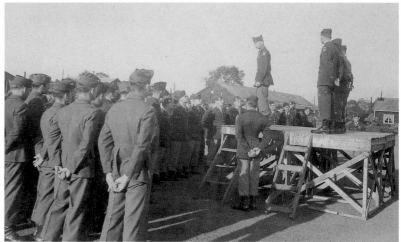

General Gavin speaks to paratroopers in England prior to the invasion of Normandy. *U.S. Army photograph, courtesy of the 82nd Airborne Division War Memorial Museum*

Brigadier General James M. Gavin, assistant division commander (left), and Colonel Rueben H. Tucker, commander of the 504th PIR (right), meet after the arrival of the 504th RCT in England. *U.S. Army photograph, courtesy of the 82nd Airborne Division War Memorial Museum*

A C-47 tows a Waco glider over the English countryside in a training flight in the spring of 1944. *U.S. Army photograph, courtesy of the Silent Wings Museum*

Company I, 505th PIR, at the rifle range near Camp Quorn, England, spring 1944. *Photograph courtesy of Harry Buffone*

The 505th Parachute Infantry Regiment camp located the grounds of the Quorn House on Wood Lane in Quorndon, England. *Photograph courtesy of Jerome V. Huth*

Paratroopers with the 505th PIR prepare for an inspection. *Photograph courtesy of Jerome V. Huth*

Weapons and equipment on a blanket ready for an inspection. *Photograph courtesy of Jerome V. Huth*

Thompson submachine guns, M1 carbines, and M1 rifles ready for inspection. *Photograph courtesy of Jerome V. Huth*

Crates of ammunition are unloaded from a 2½-ton truck in preparation for making ammunition bundles. *Photograph courtesy of Jerome V. Huth*

Troopers work to prepare an equipment bundle prior to leaving for the airfields, May 1944. *Photograph courtesy of Jerome V. Huth*

Prior to moving to the airfield in May 1944, 505th PIR troopers finish making an ammunition bundle. *Photograph courtesy of Jerome V. Huth*

Paratroopers at Camp Quorn stand in line to board buses to their airfield, May 1944. *Photograph courtesy of Jerome V. Huth*

Troopers load equipment bundles on a C-47 prior to the Normandy jump. *Photograph courtesy of Jerome V. Huth*

Troopers bow their heads in prayer at a religious service on June 5, 1944. *U.S. Army photograph, courtesy of the 82nd Airborne Division War Memorial Museum*

Troopers with the 508th PIR are given V-mail blanks to write their last letters home before the invasion of Normandy, June 5, 1944. *U.S. Army photograph, courtesy of the National Archives*

Paratroopers with the 508th PIR move out of the hanger at Saltby Airfield in preparation for boarding their aircraft, June 5, 1944. *Photographic still of U.S. Army combat camera film, courtesy of Tyler Alberts and www.combatreels.com*

In the growing darkness of June 5, 1944, 508th PIR troopers march to their aircraft. *Photographic still of U.S. Army combat camera film, courtesy of Tyler Alberts and www.combatreels.com*

Paratroopers at Saltby Airfield form up in their respective sticks to board their aircraft, June 5, 1944. *Photographic still of U.S. Army combat camera film, courtesy of Tyler Alberts and www.combatreels.com*

Troopers begin to board their aircraft at Saltby Airfield, June 5, 1944. *Photographic still of U.S. Army combat camera film, courtesy of Tyler Alberts and www.combatreels.com*

Two troopers perform a last-minute equipment check before boarding their C-47 in the fading light, June 5, 1944. *Photographic still of U.S. Army combat camera film, courtesy of Tyler Alberts and www.combatreels.com*

The 1st Battalion, 505th PIR Pathfinder Team shortly before boarding their plane for Normandy, June 5, 1944. *U.S. Army photograph, courtesy of Bob Murphy*

The 2nd Battalion, 505th PIR Pathfinder Team prior to boarding their C-47 for Normandy, June 5, 1944. *U.S. Army photograph, courtesy of Julius Eisner*

The 3rd Battalion, 505th PIR Pathfinder Team prior to boarding their aircraft for Normandy, June 5, 1944. *U.S. Army photograph, courtesy of the 82nd Airborne Division War Memorial Museum*

Chapter 9

"ALMIGHTY GOD, OUR SONS, PRIDE OF OUR NATION, THIS DAY HAVE SET UPON A MIGHTY ENDEAVOR"

On the night of June 5, 378 planes carrying the parachute elements of the 82nd Airborne Division began lifting off from their airfields in northern England headed for Normandy, France. With the 505th PIR in the lead, followed by the 508th PIR, and finally the 507th PIR, the huge armada swept over the English countryside, then southwest out over the English Channel at Weymouth, to a beacon from a submarine used as a checkpoint, and then swung left toward the west coast of the Cotentin Peninsula of Normandy. As the serials of thirty-six to forty-five planes approached the coast, a cloudbank obscured landmarks, and about three or four miles inland, enemy antiaircraft fire rose up to meet the low-flying aircraft.

The only pathfinder teams that landed on their drop zone and were able to set up their Eureka direction-finding equipment and lights were the three experienced 505th pathfinder teams. As a result, the 505th PIR was the only regiment of both the 82nd and 101st Airborne Divisions to have an accurate drop, with most of the regiment landing within a few miles of Ste.-Mère-Église. The other pathfinder teams from the 507th and 508th were either dropped in the wrong locations or were unable to set up their equipment because of enemy fire on their drop zones. The 508th PIR troopers were scattered over an area around their drop zone, with a number of sticks landing in the flooded areas of the Merderet and Douve Rivers. The 507th PIR was the most widely scattered, with only 2 of 117 sticks landing on the drop zone. Many came down in the flooded area of the Merderet River, and others as far away as Graignes, southeast of Carentan. Because the paratroopers of both divisions were widely scattered, the German commanders were unable to determine the main objectives of the paratroopers, and were hesitant to commit forces to a counterattack as a result. In the darkness, small groups of paratroopers from different units began to get together and form ad hoc units, as troopers tried to determine their locations.

That night, June 6, 1944, President Franklin D. Roosevelt addressed the nation and the world in a broadcast radio address.

LAST NIGHT WHEN I SPOKE WITH YOU ABOUT THE FALL OF ROME, I KNEW AT THAT MOMENT THAT TROOPS OF THE UNITED STATES AND OUR ALLIES WERE CROSSING THE CHANNEL IN ANOTHER AND GREATER OPERATION. IT HAS COME TO PASS WITH SUCCESS THUS

FAR. AND SO, IN THIS POIGNANT HOUR, I ASK YOU TO JOIN WITH ME IN PRAYER:

ALMIGHTY GOD: OUR SONS, PRIDE OF OUR NATION, THIS DAY HAVE SET UPON A MIGHTY ENDEAVOR, A STRUGGLE TO PRESERVE OUR REPUBLIC, OUR RELIGION, AND OUR CIVILIZATION, AND TO SET FREE A SUFFERING HUMANITY. LEAD THEM STRAIGHT AND TRUE; GIVE STRENGTH TO THEIR ARMS, STOUTNESS TO THEIR HEARTS, STEADFASTNESS IN THEIR FAITH. THEY WILL NEED THY BLESSINGS. THEIR ROAD WILL BE LONG AND HARD. FOR THE ENEMY IS STRONG. HE MAY HURL BACK OUR FORCES. SUCCESS MAY NOT COME WITH RUSHING SPEED, BUT WE SHALL RETURN AGAIN AND AGAIN; AND WE KNOW THAT BY THY GRACE, AND BY THE RIGHTEOUSNESS OF OUR CAUSE, OUR SONS WILL TRIUMPH. . . .

Aircraft flying in the nine-plane V-of-V formation that carried one rifle company. A serial of thirty-six or forty-five planes carried a battalion. *Photographic still of U.S. Army combat camera film, courtesy of Tyler Alberts and www.combatreels.com*

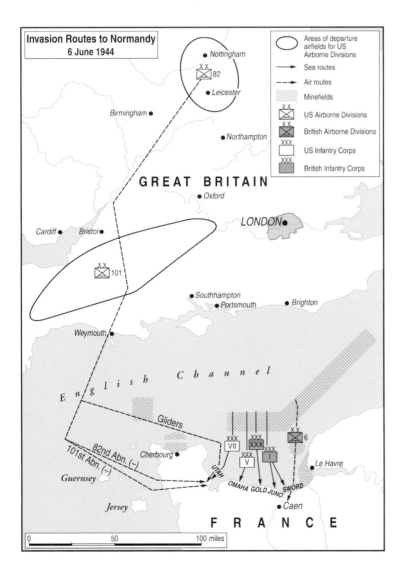

One of the thirty-six paratroopers of the 82nd Airborne Division who drowned in the flooded areas of the Merderet and Douve Rivers. *U.S. Army photograph, courtesy of the 82nd Airborne Division War Memorial Museum*

Wreckage of a C-47 in a Norman field. *U.S. Army photograph, courtesy of the 82nd Airborne Division War Memorial Museum*

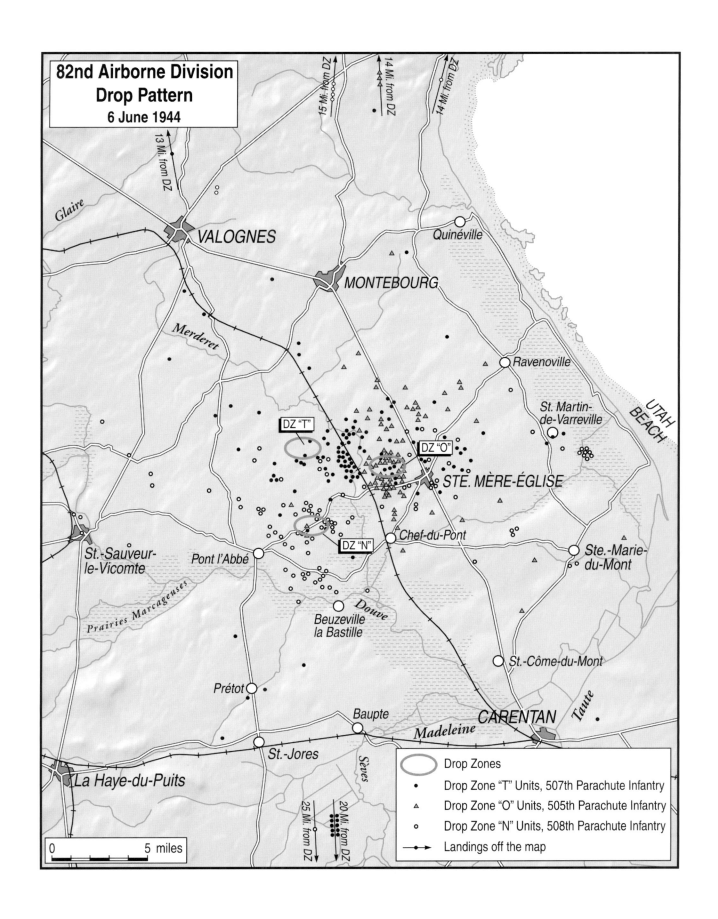

82nd Airborne Division Drop Pattern
6 June 1944

15 Mi. from DZ
14 Mi. from DZ
14 Mi. from DZ
13 Mi. from DZ

Glaire

VALOGNES

Quinéville

MONTEBOURG

Merderet

Ravenoville

St. Martin-de-Varreville

DZ "T"

DZ "O"

UTAH BEACH

STE. MÈRE-ÉGLISE

St.-Sauveur-le-Vicomte

Pont l'Abbé

DZ "N"

Chef-du-Pont

Ste.-Marie-du-Mont

Prairies Marcageuses

Douve

Beuzeville la Bastille

St.-Côme-du-Mont

Prétot

Baupte

CARENTAN

Taute

Madeleine

St.-Jores

Seves

La Haye-du-Puits

25 Mi. from DZ
20 Mi. from DZ

⬭	Drop Zones
•	Drop Zone "T" Units, 507th Parachute Infantry
△	Drop Zone "O" Units, 505th Parachute Infantry
○	Drop Zone "N" Units, 508th Parachute Infantry
•→	Landings off the map

0   5 miles

"WHEREVER YOU LAND, MAKE YOUR WAY TO STE.-MÈRE-ÉGLISE, AND TOGETHER WE WILL RAISE THIS FLAG"

After landing, the veterans of the 505th PIR began assembling west of Ste.-Mère-Église. Lieutenant Colonel Krause's 3rd Battalion moved into the town, while Lieutenant Colonel Benjamin H. Vandervoort's 2nd Battalion moved toward Neuville-au-Plain about a mile north of Ste.-Mère-Église to block German forces that would surely move south along the main Cherbourg-to-Paris highway, and Major Frederick Kellam's 1st Battalion moved west to the eastern end of the La Fière causeway along the Merderet River.

Because some of their sticks didn't hit the drop zone, the veteran troopers of the 3rd Battalion converged on Ste.-Mère-Église from all directions. Every trooper in the battalion probably remembered Lieutenant Colonel Krause's sendoff talk the previous evening: "Wherever you land, make your way to Ste.-Mère-Église, and together we will raise this flag . . . the same one that flew over the post office in Naples . . . over the highest building in the town."

Krause's troopers established blocking positions on all roads leading into Ste.-Mère-Église, then cleared the town after a short fight. As troopers moved through the town, they saw a number of dead troop-ers still in their harnesses, hanging from trees and overhead electrical and telephone wires. The dead troopers, from Company F, 505th PIR, had dropped into the town square as a raging fire engulfed an adjacent house. Illuminated by the flames, the troopers were shot as they struggled to get out of their harnesses.

At 4:00 a.m. on June 6, 1944, fifty-two CG-4A Waco gliders carrying Batteries A and B, 80th Airborne Antiaircraft (Antitank) Battalion, most elements of the 82nd Airborne Division Headquarters and Headquarters Company; Headquarters and Headquarters Battery, Division Artillery, and the 82nd Signal Company, began landing west of Ste.-Mère-Église in the predawn darkness. The small fields were lined with hedgerows, where trees and heavy undergrowth sat atop dirt and stone embankments four to six feet high. The result was crash landings, which caused a significant number of casualties. Some gliders released off course, but six 57mm antitank guns were recovered and available for the defense of the Ste.-Mère-Église area.

The commander of the 505th PIR, Colonel Bill Ekman, had landed northeast of Ste.-Mère-Église and at dawn found Vandervoort's 2nd Battalion en route to Neuville-au-Plain. Not aware that the 3rd Battalion

An aerial view of the town of Ste.-Mère-Église, France, facing south, with the N-13 Paris-to-Cherbourg highway running through the town. This crossroads town was a chokepoint for German forces moving to attack the Utah Beach landings from the west or north. *U.S. Army photograph, courtesy of the National Archives*

had taken Ste.-Mère-Église, Ekman directed Vandervoort to take his battalion south to help secure the town. Vandervoort left one platoon of Company D at Neuville-au-Plain to block the road.

Upon arriving in Ste.-Mère-Église, Vandervoort found the town in the hands of the 3rd Battalion. Krause and Vandervoort decided to divide the defense of the town, with the 3rd Battalion defending the south and west, and the 2nd Battalion defending the north and east sides of the perimeter.

Later that morning Ste.-Mère-Église came under attack by German forces south and east, and afterward west of the town. The lone Company D platoon with the help of one of the 57mm antitank guns held off a German regiment, reinforced with artillery and self-propelled guns until late in the afternoon, when it withdrew to Ste.-Mère-Église with the help of a platoon from Company E, 505th.

Aerial photo of Ste.-Mère-Église (upper left) and the hamlet of Fauville (lower center) to the south. *U.S. Army Air Corps photograph*

A dead enemy soldier, killed in the German attack on Ste.-Mère-Église. *Photograph courtesy of Harry Buffone*

A dead 82nd Airborne paratrooper, killed while attempting to retrieve gasoline and other supplies from a glider. *U.S. Army photograph, courtesy of the 82nd Airborne Division War Memorial Museum*

Troopers with the 505th PIR run for the door of the church at Ste.-Mère-Église as enemy artillery pounds the town, June 6, 1944. *U.S. Army photograph, courtesy of the 82nd Airborne Division War Memorial Museum*

Chapter 11

"THIS WAS ONE OF THE TOUGHEST DAYS OF MY LIFE"

West of Ste.-Mère-Église, the 1st Battalion, 505th, led by Company A, moved toward the eastern end of the causeway that crossed the Merderet River at the La Fière Manoir. Simultaneously, several groups of paratroopers from the 507th PIR and 508th PIR that had been dropped into the flooded area of the Merderet River and to the east of the river converged on the La Fière Causeway as a means of getting to the west side of the river, where their regimental objectives were located.

A platoon of German soldiers with four machine guns defended the Manoir, the fields to the east, and the east-west road leading from Ste.-Mère-Église to the Manoir. Company A, 505th, as well as a group of Company G, 507th, troopers and a couple of groups of 508th troopers each independently approached the Manoir from the east just south of the main east-west road. German machine guns stopped the advance, causing one platoon of Company A to be sent north across the road and then west to approach the Manoir from the north. The group of Company G, 507th, troopers swung south and then west to the bank of the Merderet River, then north to the Manoir, knocking out the German machine gun that held up the initial advance. The rest of Company A, 505th, also moved south and then west, approaching the Manoir from the southeast, while the 508th groups approached from the east over a couple of Roman burial grounds.

After a short series of firefights in and around the Manoir buildings, the Germans were all killed or captured and the Manoir secured. The 507th troopers crossed the causeway and proceeded to join Lieutenant Colonel Charles Timmes' force of mostly paratroopers from the 507th, dug-in at an orchard east of Amfresville. Some Company B, 508th, troopers crossed a short time later and turned south along the road on the west side of the Merderet River. There, they encountered a large German force, supported by French-made Renault and Hotchkiss tanks, that forced them to retreat across the flooded Merderet River under heavy fire. The German force then moved north to Cauquigny, near the western end of the causeway, where it forced a small group of 507th troopers to retreat to Timmes' orchard.

A German force of three French tanks and about one hundred fifty infantry then moved across the causeway toward the La Fière Manoir, where Company A, 505th, supported by the 1st Battalion, 505th, destroyed the three tanks with bazooka and 57mm antitank gun fire and killed or wounded most of the enemy infantry. Private Marcus Heim, a loader for one of the two Company A, 505th, bazooka teams that had knocked out the tanks at almost point-blank range, said, "This was one of the toughest days of my life. Why we were not injured or killed only the good Lord knows."

The Manoir house at La Fière as viewed from the southeast. *U.S. Army photograph, courtesy of the 82nd Airborne Division War Memorial Museum*

The Manoir outbuildings and the approach used by the 508th PIR troopers to enter the Manoir grounds. *U.S. Army photograph, courtesy of the 82nd Airborne Division War Memorial Museum*

The Roman burial mounds located east of the Manoir house. *U.S. Army photograph, courtesy of the 82nd Airborne Division War Memorial Museum*

The Manoir viewed from the Merderet River bridge to the northwest. *U.S. Army photograph, courtesy of the 82nd Airborne Division War Memorial Museum*

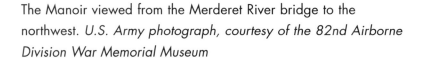

The Merderet River bridge at the east end of the La Fière Causeway, looking west. *Photograph courtesy of the 82nd Airborne Division War Memorial Museum*

Three French tanks of the German 100th Panzer Training and Replacement Battalion lie destroyed at the east end of the La Fière Causeway. *Photographic still from U.S. Army motion picture, courtesy of the Martin K. A. Morgan and the National Archives*

Chapter 12

"I THINK IT'S TIME TO GET OUR WAR STARTED"

On the morning of June 6, 1944, ad hoc groups of paratroopers, primarily from the 507th and 508th PIRs, who had been scattered over the Cotentin Peninsula, ambushed and attacked German forces. That morning, a small group of paratroopers, led by Lieutenant Malcolm Brannen, ambushed and killed General Wilhelm Falley, the commander of the German 91st Airlanding Division, a unit specifically trained to counter enemy airborne landings.

Private David Jones, with Headquarters Company, 1st Battalion, 508th, had field-stripped his M1 rifle and was cleaning it after landing in a flooded area the previous night. "No sooner did I get the M1 all laid out and drying nicely, someone yells, 'Tanks!' I finally got my weapon reassembled, and watching those tanks rattling up that causeway towards the farmhouse that we were hiding behind gave no cause for celebration.

"Now these were French Renault tanks, probably the smallest tanks used during the entire war. But to me, they were larger than life. I remember the lead tank had its hatch open and the black-capped tank commander was exposed from the waist up, hands resting outside the turret. I can't explain why in the world I said it, but to my nearest companion I said, 'I think it's time to get our war started.'"

Two groups of mostly 507th troopers led by Lieutenant Colonel Edwin Ostberg and Lieutenant Colonel Arthur Maloney attacked Chef-du-Pont, where a second causeway across the Merderet River near the confluence with the Douve River provided a means for German forces intent on attacking the landings at Utah Beach. After an all-day fight, the Germans dug in along the causeway were killed or routed. Other groups of 507th troopers attacked Amfresville, but were forced to withdraw from the town.

Three groups of paratroopers, mostly with the 508th, that had landed west of the Merderet River, were ordered to move to Hill 30 on the west bank of the Merderet River between the La Fière and Chef-du-Pont Causeways, where they joined forces with Lieutenant Colonel Thomas Shanley.

That evening 176 gliders carrying Battery C, 80th Airborne Antiaircraft (Antitank) Battalion, the 319th and 320th Glider Field Artillery Battalions, elements of the 307th Medical Company, along with vehicles, ammunition, water, and food, landed southeast of Ste.-Mère-Église as German guns on a wooded hill to the north took the slow-moving gliders and their tugs under fire. An armored task force of the division, commanded by Colonel Edson Raff, which had lost three Sherman tanks earlier in an attempt to break through to the paratroopers defending Ste.-Mère-Église, could only watch as the gliders were shot up as they landed.

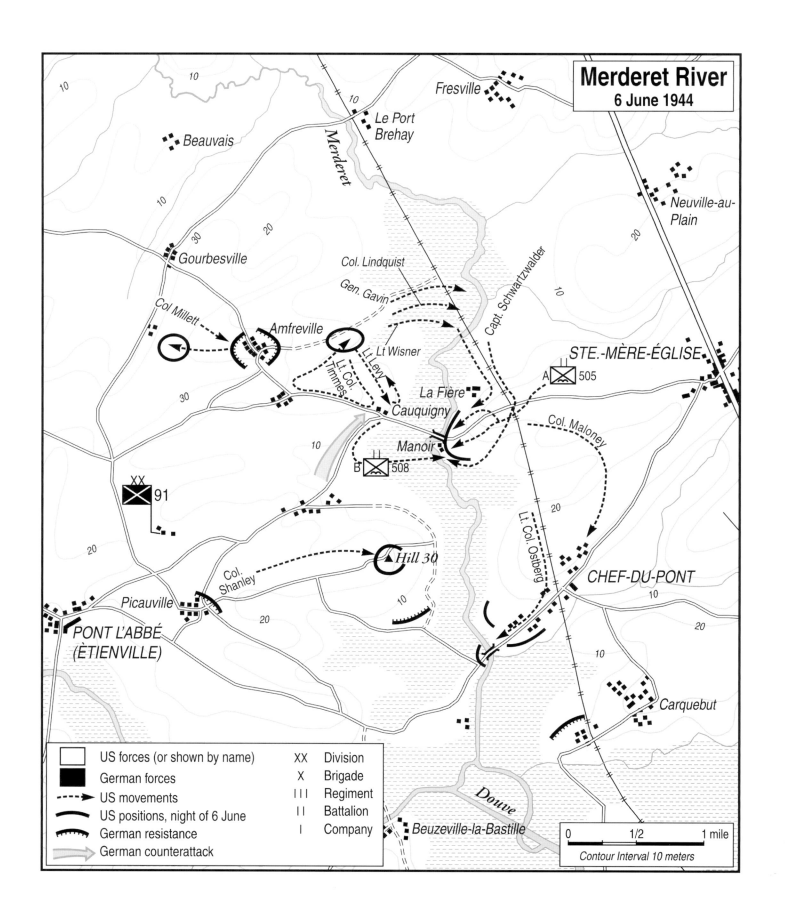

Merderet River
6 June 1944

Fresville

Le Port
Brehay

Beauvais

Merderet

Neuville-au-
Plain

Gourbesville

Col. Lindquist

Gen. Gavin

Capt. Schwartzwalder

Col Millett

Amfreville

STE.-MÈRE-ÉGLISE

Lt Wisner

A ⊠ 505

Lt. Col.
Timmes

Lt. Levy

La Fière

Cauquigny

Col. Maloney

Manoir

B ⊠ 508

XX
⊠ 91

Lt. Col. Ostberg

Hill 30

CHEF-DU-PONT

Col.
Shanley

Picauville

PONT L'ABBÉ
(ÈTIENVILLE)

Carquebut

Douve

Beuzeville-la-Bastille

	US forces (or shown by name)	XX	Division
	German forces	X	Brigade
	US movements	III	Regiment
	US positions, night of 6 June	II	Battalion
	German resistance	I	Company
	German counterattack		

0   1/2   1 mile

Contour Interval 10 meters

Paratroopers move cautiously through the dense hedgerow or bocage of the Norman countryside. *Photographic still of U.S. Army combat camera film, courtesy of Tyler Alberts and www.combatreels.com*

Death stalked the hedgerows as paratroopers fought against German forces on June 6, 1944. Private Robert B. White, with Company A, 508th, stands over a dead German. *Photograph courtesy of Henry LeFebre and Robert B. White*

A group of paratroopers dropped near Utah Beach move through the town of St.-Marcouf on the way to find their units. *Photographic still of U.S. Army combat camera film, courtesy of Tyler Alberts and www.combatreels.com*

An aerial view of Chef-du-Pont and the causeway over the Merderet River. *U.S. Army photograph, courtesy of the 82nd Airborne Division War Memorial Museum*

The three rifle companies of the 1st Battalion, 325th GIR, line up beside their assigned gliders, June 6, 1944. *U.S. Army photograph, courtesy of the 82nd Airborne Division War Memorial Museum*

Troopers stack their weapons before they load their gear on their glider, June 6, 1944. *U.S. Army photograph, courtesy of the 82nd Airborne Division War Memorial Museum*

As fighting rages in Normandy, troopers of the 1st Battalion, 325th GIR, loaded down with their weapons and gear, move to their British Horsa gliders on June 6, 1944. *U.S. Army photograph, courtesy of the 82nd Airborne Division War Memorial Museum*

Medics assigned to the 1st Battalion, 325th GIR, rest by their Horsa glider, June 6, 1944. *U.S. Army photograph, courtesy of the 82nd Airborne Division War Memorial Museum*

Chapter 13

"I DON'T KNOW OF A BETTER PLACE TO DIE"

On the morning of June 7, 1944, the 325th GIR and Company A, 307th Airborne Engineer Battalion, took off from airfields in England in four serials, a total of two hundred British Horsa and American CG-4A gliders. The serials landed at 7:00 a.m., 7:10 a.m., 9:00 a.m., and 9:10 a.m. Enemy antiaircraft fire was not as deadly as the anti-landing obstacles and the small, hedgerow-lined fields. Out of forty-eight huge, British-built Horsa gliders used, sixteen were destroyed and seventeen damaged, with thirty-two men killed. The American-built CG-4A Waco gliders fared somewhat better, with 37 destroyed and another 79 damaged, out of the 152 employed. Only one fatality occurred among those brought in by the Waco gliders. A total of 172 officers and men were wounded or injured during the approach and landings.

As this was occurring, savage fighting was taking place on and around Hill 30 on the west bank of the Merderet River, where paratroopers mostly of the 508th PIR fought off repeated attacks from three sides. To the north, Lieutenant Colonel Timmes' force, mainly composed of 507th PIR troopers, held an orchard on the west side of the Merderet River north of the La Fière Causeway, effectively tying down a considerable force of enemy troops.

At dawn, following a massive, hour-long artillery and mortar barrage against the eastern end of the La Fière Causeway, the Germans launched an infantry attack, supported by two tanks, against the 1st Battalion, 505th PIR, primarily troopers with Company A. If German forces could take the causeway, they could push east against the hard-pressed defenders of Ste.-Mère-Église or against elements of the 4th Infantry Division moving inland from Utah Beach. A 57mm antitank gun knocked out the two tanks, but the German infantry came on and were met with a withering fire from the veteran paratroopers. The Germans pulled back and blasted the defenders again with artillery and heavy mortars. Their infantry attacked again, only to be thrown back once more. The Germans fired another heavy barrage of artillery and mortars before attacking across the causeway for a third time.

Sergeant William D. Owens, with Company A, the senior NCO in his platoon after several other officers and NCOs had been killed or wounded, sent his runner, Corporal Darrell J. Franks, to find the company commander, Lieutenant John J. "Red" Dolan. Owens told Franks to ask if they should pull back; his platoon was down to around fifteen men and almost out of ammunition. Franks returned a short time later with Dolan's answer scribbled on a scrap of paper. It read, "I don't know of a better place than this to die."

Just as Owens and the others in his platoon thought that they might be overrun and wiped out by the German infantry, he saw the enemy waving a Red Cross flag and ceased firing. Owens got his troopers to stop firing, and the enemy picked up their wounded and retreated across the causeway, ending the threat.

Glider infantrymen with the 1st Battalion, 325th GIR, carrying their personal weapons board their Horsa glider, June 7, 1944. *U.S. Army photograph, courtesy of the 82nd Airborne Division War Memorial Museum*

Glider troopers with the 325th GIR wait for takeoff in their CG-4A Waco glider, June 7, 1944. *U.S. Army photograph, courtesy of the 82nd Airborne Division War Memorial Museum*

Waiting for takeoff in their Horsa glider are infantrymen of the 1st Battalion, 325th GIR, June 7, 1944. *U.S. Army photograph, courtesy of the 82nd Airborne Division War Memorial Museum*

C-47s and their gliders flying over Utah Beach, June 7, 1944. *U.S. Army photograph, courtesy of the Silent Wings Museum*

C-47 aircraft tow CG-4A gliders behind them on the way to Normandy, June 7, 1944. *U.S. Army photograph, courtesy of the 82nd Airborne Division War Memorial Museum*

Tugs release their gliders over Normandy, June 7, 1944. Several damaged or destroyed gliders may be seen on the ground, as well as U.S. Army tanks on the N-13 highway in the center of the photograph. *Photograph courtesy of the Press Association, Inc.*

The length of the shadows in this photo are an indication of the height of the hedgerows where these gliders landed and why they caused so much damage to the gliders landing on June 7, 1944. *U.S. Army photograph, courtesy of the 82nd Airborne Division War Memorial Museum*

The bodies of two paratroopers lie near a CG-4A glider, where they were retrieving supplies. *Photograph courtesy of the Silent Wings Museum*

The Rommel's Asparagus anti-glider obstacles have torn the wings on this glider, damaging the fuselage. *U.S. Army photograph, courtesy of the National Archives*

This Horsa glider was severely damaged during its landing on June 7, 1944. *Photograph courtesy of Jerome V. Huth*

Waiting for takeoff in their Horsa glider are infantrymen of the 1st Battalion, 325th GIR, June 7, 1944. *U.S. Army photograph, courtesy of the 82nd Airborne Division War Memorial Museum*

The debris of a Horsa glider that crashed during landing in the small fields of Normandy. *U.S. Army photograph, courtesy of the 82nd Airborne Division War Memorial Museum*

The bodies of Lieutenant James A. Gayley, commander of Company A, 325th GIR, and sixteen of his men, killed when their Horsa glider crashed near Hiesville, June 7, 1944. *U.S. Army photograph, courtesy of the 82nd Airborne Division War Memorial Museum*

Chapter 14

"COLONEL, AREN'T YOU GLAD WAVERLY'S ON OUR SIDE?"

On the morning of June 7, a German force of three infantry battalions, supported by self-propelled guns, and three regiments of artillery pressed toward the northern edge of Ste.-Mère-Église. A single platoon of Company D, 505th PIR, on the east side of the N-13 highway blocked the way. The troopers held off hordes of attackers, but were finally forced away from the road.

The Germans sent a self-propelled gun down the road to within fifty yards of the 2nd Battalion, 505th PIR, command post (CP), where it was engaged by a 57mm antitank gun manned by a crew under Lieutenant John C. Cliff from Battery A, 80th Airborne Antiaircraft (Antitank) Battalion. The courageous crew knocked out the vehicle with two shots through the frontal armor. Cliff's crew moved their gun up to the side of the knocked-out vehicle to gain better visibility of the road, but were hit and wounded in the process. A second German self-propelled gun moved forward unopposed, until Private John E. Atchley, with Company H, 505th PIR, gallantly manned the antitank gun and single-handedly destroyed the oncoming vehicle. This temporarily stopped the German armored threat, but not the infantry pressing in from the north in fields on each side of the road.

Lieutenant Waverly Wray, the Company D executive officer, was ordered by Lieutenant Colonel Vandervoort to counterattack the German flank. Wray led a platoon to the left flank of the enemy battalion east of the highway, the main body of which was positioned in a hedgerow-lined lane just north of the town. Wray continued into the midst of the German positions, where he killed the commander of the German battalion and his staff.

Wray then returned and positioned his platoon at the end of the lane on the flank of the German battalion and ordered a .30-caliber machine gun to fire down the lane as a 60mm mortar methodically walked rounds along the lane. This drove the Germans out of the lane and into the fields on both sides, where the rest of the platoon took them under fire. The result was the destruction of the now leaderless battalion and a temporary halt in the German advance. Later that afternoon, after American tanks arrived at Ste.-Mère-Église, a platoon of Company E, 505th PIR, along with two of the tanks launched an attack on the flank of the German battalion west of the highway, destroying it as well, ending the threat to the town.

Early the next morning, Wray took Vandervoort to the site of his remarkable feat. Vandervoort saw firsthand evidence of what he had been told. "The dead battalion commander and seven staff corpses were still there. It had to be an eerie shock to any German visiting the place. Across the field were two dead Schmeisser-armed Grenadiers—both shot in the head.

"John Rabig, Waverly's first sergeant, summed up Wray's performance the next day with the comment, 'Colonel, aren't you glad Waverly's on our side?' Waverly's unique performance set him apart as an authentic hero, but he never showed it in his demeanor. He was nominated for the Congressional Medal of Honor. The recommendation was downgraded and awarded as a DSC. Those who knew him best think of Waverly W. Wray as the 82nd Airborne Division's undiscovered World War II equivalent of Sergeant Alvin C. York. He stands tall among those who made the great invasion succeed."

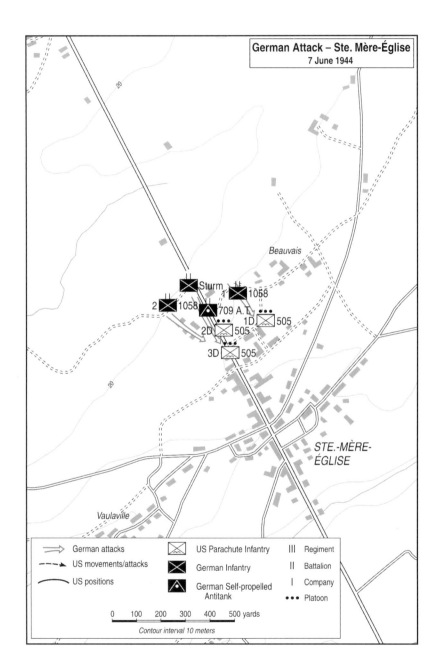

German Attack – Ste. Mère-Église
7 June 1944

Beauvais

Sturm

1 1058

2 1058

709 A.T.

1D ••• 505

2D 505

3D 505

STE.-MÈRE-ÉGLISE

Vaulaville

⇒ German attacks	⊠ US Parachute Infantry	III Regiment
---► US movements/attacks	◼ German Infantry	II Battalion
⌒ US positions	◢ German Self-propelled Antitank	I Company
		••• Platoon

0 100 200 300 400 500 yards

Contour interval 10 meters

The German self-propelled gun destroyed by Battery A, 80th Airborne Antiaircraft (Antitank) Battalion, on the northern edge of Ste.-Mère-Église, June 7, 1944. *Photograph courtesy of Colonel Robert M. Piper*

The 57mm antitank gun sits beside the destroyed self-propelled gun shown in the preceding photograph, shortly after the action by Private John Atchley, Company H, 505th PIR, to destroy the second self-propelled gun shrouded in smoke in the distance. *Photograph courtesy of the 82nd Airborne Division War Memorial Museum*

Looking south toward Ste.-Mère-Église, the German self-propelled gun single-handedly destroyed by Private John E. Atchley is in the foreground. The other destroyed self-propelled gun knocked out a gun crew from Battery A, 80th AA Battalion, and the 57mm antitank gun that destroyed both vehicles can be seen in the distance. *U.S. Army photograph courtesy of the 82nd Airborne Division War Memorial Museum*

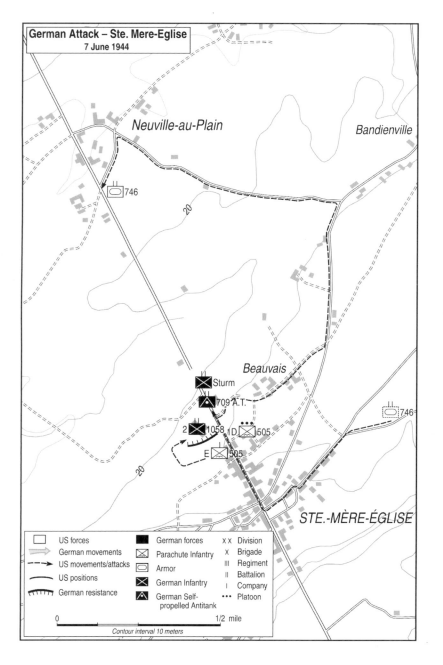

Three Company D, 505th PIR officers, left to right: Lieutenants O. B. Carr, Tom McClean, and Waverly Wray. *Photograph courtesy of V. P. DeWailly*

An 81mm mortar is fired by a crew with Headquarters Company, 2nd Battalion, 505th PIR, in defense of Ste.-Mère-Église, June 7, 1944. *Photographic still of U.S. Army combat camera film, courtesy of Tyler Alberts and www.combatreels.com*

German POWs captured by the 505th PIR are marched to Utah Beach for evacuation, June 8, 1944. *U.S. Army photograph, courtesy of the 82nd Airborne Division War Memorial Museum*

The result of German shelling of Ste.-Mère-Église, June 8, 1944. *U.S. Army photograph, courtesy of the 82nd Airborne Division War Memorial Museum*

A German Marder self-propelled gun sits on the side of the N-13 highway north of Ste.-Mère-Église, one of the casualties of the fighting on June 6 and 7, 1944. *U.S. Army photograph, courtesy of the 82nd Airborne Division War Memorial Museum*

The N-13 highway runs through a shell-torn Ste.-Mère-Église, June 8, 1944. *U.S. Army photograph, courtesy of the 82nd Airborne Division War Memorial Museum*

Chapter 15

"VAN, DON'T KILL THEM ALL. SAVE A FEW FOR INTERROGATION"

During the night of June 7–8, seventy men and officers from the 508th PIR force commanded by Lieutenant Colonel Shanley moved down Hill 30 and established a roadblock on the western end of the Chef-du-Pont Causeway. A group of about two hundred troopers, commanded by the CO of the 507th PIR, Colonel George V. Millett Jr., that had fought off several strong attacks that day northwest of Amfresville, was joined by another group of two hundred troopers that had moved from their positions east of Amfresville.

Shortly after midnight, the 505th PIR attacked northward from the Ste.-Mère-Église area to drive toward Montebourg Station and Le Ham. After sunrise on the morning of June 8, when General Gavin viewed the fields north of Ste.-Mère-Église strewn with hundreds of German corpses, he jokingly said to Vandervoort, "Van, don't kill them all. Save a few for interrogation."

That day, the Germans attacked Hill 30 from three sides, but were thrown back in vicious, often hand-to-hand fighting. The troopers on Hill 30 were running low on ammunition and had practically no medical supplies to treat the wounded. The troopers at the roadblock were forced away, but a combat patrol returned after dark to reestablish the block in brutal hand-to-hand, no-prisoners-taken combat.

On the night of June 8–9, over four hundred troopers, mostly from the 507th PIR, led by Colonel Millett moved east to link up with Timmes' force at the orchard north of the western end of the La Fière Causeway. During the predawn hours, the front half of the column of Millett's group ran into a large German force and was captured.

Also, that night the 1st Battalion, 325th GIR, was sent across a ford in the Merderet River north of the La Fière Causeway to attack the western end of the causeway from the rear. Company A blocked the main road from Amfresville, to bar German forces that might attack from the west. Company B moved east and ran into a strong German force in an orchard north of the main road from Cauquigny to Amfresville, where eighteen men were killed and many wounded. South of the road, Company C came upon the rear of a German artillery position in a field across a sunken road that ran southwest from the main road. Caught by surprise, the German crews waved white flags. As the company started across the road to take the German prisoners, they were hit with enfilade machine gun fire from machine guns firing down the sunken road from both flanks. The platoon in the center made it to the field beyond only to be decimated. The survivors pulled back under withering fire to a ditch that lined the sunken road.

As German infantry closed in from the flank, Private First Class Charles DeGlopper stood up in the middle of the road and began firing burst after burst from his Browning Automatic Rifle (BAR) to cover the retreat of the surviving members of his platoon from the sunken road. Despite being hit several times and mortally wounded, DeGlopper continued to fire until he was killed outright. Around DeGlopper's body, the ground was strewn with dead Germans and many automatic weapons and machine guns. DeGlopper was later posthumously awarded the Congressional Medal of Honor.

The survivors of the 1st Battalion, 325th GIR, withdrew to join the forces in Timmes' orchard.

Paratroopers with the 505th PIR check a map as they move down a country lane lined with hedgerows and trees on both sides. *U.S. Army photograph, courtesy of the 82nd Airborne Division War Memorial Museum*

During the advance north from Ste.-Mère-Église, 505th PIR troopers move along a hedgerow-lined road. *Photographic still of U.S. Army combat camera film, courtesy of Tyler Alberts and*

Map

Ecausseville and Le Ham
8–11 June 1944

le Ht. Gaillon
le Guinguette
l'Abbaye
St. Floxel
St. Cyr
MONTEBOURG
la Rue St. Claire
ELEMENTS OF 709TH AND 243 DIVISIONS AND STURM BN
Martinvast
Eroudeville
la Lande Magnon
8–12
Joganville
la Corneillerie
la Basse Emondeville
Montebourg Station
Ecausseville
Emondeville
1 ⊠ 505
la Lande
2 ⊠ 505
82 X 4
Magneville
le Ham 2 ⊠ 325
la Vallee
le Ht. du Ham
Conneville
le Frene Bisson
le Goulet
21 ⊠ 325
Merderet
21 ⊠ 505
June 8
FRESVILLE
to Ste Mère Église
Grainville
2 ⊠ 505
le Val
la Gare
le Port Brehay
3 ⊠ 505
les Marais

US forward positions 8 June — US forces (by June 10) — XX Division
US forward positions 9 June — US positions (June 8–9) — X Brigade
US forward positions 10 June — German resistance — III Regiment
Position of 2/325, 11 June — US movements/attacks — II Battalion
0   1/2   1 mile
Contour interval 10 meters

Troopers with the 505th PIR move carefully across a pasture toward a hedgerow. *Photographic still of U.S. Army combat camera film, courtesy of Tyler Alberts and www.combatreels.com*

Colonel William E. Ekman (second from left), commander of the 505th PIR, members of his staff, and two German POWs carrying the regimental SCR-300 radio and other gear. *Photograph courtesy of Les Cruise*

Engineers with Company B, 307th Airborne Engineer Battalion, sweep the area for landmines near the railroad tracks in Fresville, France. *U.S. Army photograph, courtesy of the 82nd Airborne Division War Memorial Museum*

A German Marder self-propelled gun knocked out by the 82nd Airborne Division. *U.S. Army photograph, courtesy of the 82nd Airborne Division War Memorial Museum*

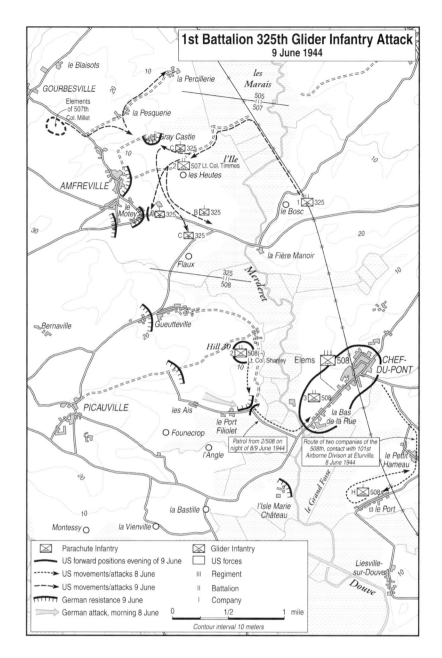

1st Battalion 325th Glider Infantry Attack
9 June 1944

A trooper with the 325th GIR aims his M1 rifle over a Norman hedgerow. *U.S. Army photograph, courtesy of the 82nd Airborne Division War Memorial Museum*

Private First Class Charles N. DeGlopper, posthumously awarded the Congressional Medal of Honor for action on June 9, 1944. *U.S. Army photograph, courtesy of the 82nd Airborne Division War Memorial Museum*

Chapter 16

"FOLLOW ME!"

After a heavy artillery barrage, the 2nd Battalion, 401st GIR, attached to the 325th GIR as its third battalion, made a frontal attack across the La Fière Causeway against a crossfire of German machine guns firing from the west bank of the Merderet River and straight down the road at the charging glider troopers. Enemy artillery and heavy mortars mercilessly pounded the causeway as the 325th troopers moved forward. Only a small number of the first two rifle companies made it to the west end of the causeway. The few who did, knocked out the German machine guns firing down the causeway and began working to the north and south to clear the western bank of enemy. The majority of the 2nd Battalion, 401st GIR, was pinned down on the causeway, lying flat on both shoulders of the causeway in an attempt to avoid enemy machine gun fire.

Three knocked-out German light tanks and an American Sherman tank that had thrown a tread when it ran over an antitank mine blocked the road. Generals Ridgway and Gavin were on the scene in the middle of the heavy fire. Ridgway helped get a cable on the Sherman tank to tow it out of the way to open the road.

At about the time the roadblock was cleared for the glider troopers, Gavin told Captain Robert Rae, who was commanding a composite company of 507th paratroopers that was held in reserve, that the attack looked as if it was faltering and that it had to go forward. With that, Rae and his men dashed across the causeway, picking up glider troopers on the causeway who joined the charge.

The attack carried across the causeway, and the bridgehead was expanded, linking up with Timmes' 507th PIR troopers in the orchard and with the 508th PIR defenders on Hill 30. Late that afternoon, Germans hit the bridgehead with several fierce counterattacks, each of which was repulsed. The 82nd Airborne elements west of the Merderet River were relieved the following morning by elements of the U.S. 90th Infantry Division.

On the morning of June 10, troopers mistakenly dropped near Graignes, southeast of Carentan, were attacked by a regiment-sized kampfgruppe of the 17th SS Panzer Grenadier Division. The 173 troopers holding the town, mostly from the 3rd Battalion, 507th, inflicted heavy casualties on the enemy.

That same day, northwest of Ste.-Mère-Église, the 1st and 2nd Battalions of the 505th PIR drove north to capture Montebourg Station and turned toward Le Ham. The 2nd Battalion, 505th, reached the edge of Le Ham, but was ordered to withdraw after savage fighting.

The next morning the 2nd Battalion, 325th GIR, attached to the 505th PIR, attacked and captured Le Ham in the face of heavy enemy opposition. Beginning that Sunday morning, the troopers at Graignes were attacked heavily throughout the day and into the night. The survivors infiltrated out of the town and into the inundated areas under cover of darkness, after practically exhausting their ammunition. German losses were heavy and the SS took revenge, massacring the wounded troopers, medics, and the battalion surgeon; twenty-four in all. They also destroyed the church and most of the houses, as well as executing a number of the civilians for collaboration.

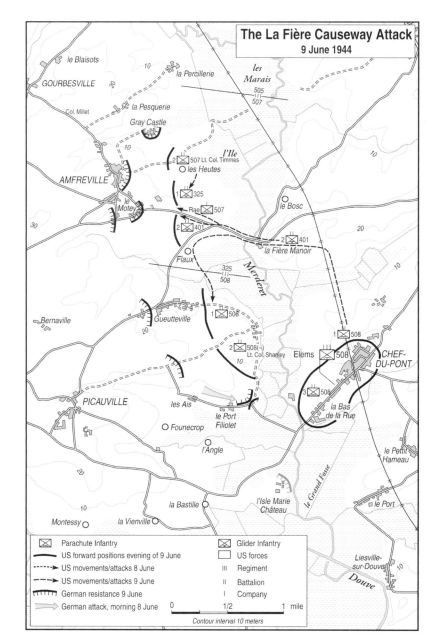

The La Fière Causeway Attack
9 June 1944

⊠ Parachute Infantry	⊠ Glider Infantry
—— US forward positions evening of 9 June	□ US forces
----- US movements/attacks 8 June	III Regiment
- - - US movements/attacks 9 June	II Battalion
⊓⊓⊓ German resistance 9 June	I Company
⟶ German attack, morning 8 June	

0   1/2   1 mile

Contour interval 10 meters

An aerial view of the La Fière Causeway looking northwest from the eastern side of the Merderet River. *U.S. Army photograph, courtesy of the 82nd Airborne Division War Memorial Museum*

Lieutenant Don Wason (left), Company G, 401st GIR, attached to the 325th GIR, was posthumously awarded the Distinguished Service Cross for single-handedly destroying the German crew that was firing a machine gun straight down the causeway. *Photograph courtesy of the 82nd Airborne Division War Memorial Museum*

An 81mm mortar crew of the 325th GIR prepares to fire in support of an attack. *U.S. Army photograph, courtesy of the 82nd Airborne Division War Memorial Museum*

Gerald Arnold (left) and Jim Schaffner (right), both with the 2nd battalion, 401st GIR, stand in front of the church at Cauquigny. Shortly after the attack on June 9,1944. German dead lie in front of the stone wall to the right. *Photograph courtesy of the 82nd Airborne Division War Memorial Museum*

Colonel Harry Lewis, commander of the 325th GIR (center, wearing eyeglasses), checks a map as one of his regiment's 81mm mortar crews stand by. *U.S. Army photograph, courtesy of the 82nd Airborne Division War Memorial Museum*

The damaged church at Cauquigny, caused by the 155mm artillery of the U.S. 90th Infantry Division's 345th Field Artillery Battalion. *Photograph courtesy of the 82nd Airborne Division War Memorial Museum*

Battery A, 320th Glider Field Artillery Battalion, hitch up one of their short-barreled 105mm howitzers in preparation for a move forward. *Photograph by Paul Speakman, courtesy of the 82nd Airborne Division War Memorial Museum*

Medics and Service Company troopers evacuate the wounded from the 505th PIR regimental aid station at Ste.-Mère-Église, while German prisoners are held in the same compound. *U.S. Army photograph, courtesy of the National Archives*

Wounded are evacuated from the 505th PIR regimental aid station in Ste.-Mère-Église. *U.S. Army photograph, courtesy of the 82nd Airborne Division War Memorial Museum*

Chapter 17

"MY GOD, MATT, CAN'T ANYTHING STOP THESE MEN?"

The 508th Regimental Combat Team made a night crossing of the Douve River and established a bridgehead at the town of Beuzeville-la-Bastille beginning at one minute after midnight on the morning of June 13. Engineers with Company A, 307th Airborne Engineer Battalion, rowed Company F, 508th PIR, across the river. Just as Company F landed, two German tanks approached on the road where a causeway crossed the river. They were both knocked out with bazookas. Then a fifteen-minute barrage by the 75mm pack howitzers of the 319th Glider Field Artillery Battalion hit the town. As this was occurring, other engineers from Company A worked to repair a blown bridge on the causeway so that the rest of the 508th PIR could cross on foot. After the barrage lifted, Company F attacked and overran the town.

The 508th PIR poured into the bridgehead, with the 1st Battalion moving southwest to capture Cretteville and then on to Coigny. The 3rd Battalion followed and pushed south in the center of the bridgehead to Taillerfer, where it formed a perimeter defense and blocked the road between Pont Auny and Hotot. The 2nd Battalion followed and advanced south on the eastern side of the bridgehead and captured Baupte after hard fighting.

The next day, north of the Douve River, with the 507th PIR on the right and the 325th GIR on the left, the division attacked west from Picauville toward St.-Sauveur-le-Vicomte, meeting stiff resistance. The following day, the 505th PIR moved through the 507th PIR to contin-ue the attack westward, with the 325th GIR advancing on its left flank. On June 16, the 505th PIR crossed the Douve River under fire and attacked St.-Sauveur-le-Vicomte and then pushed the bridgehead out to the west and north.

As General Omar Bradley watched the 505th PIR cross the Douve River and move into St. Sauveur-le-Vicomte under heavy fire, he turned to General Ridgway and said, "My God, Matt, can't anything stop these men?"

Ridgway replied, "I would rather have a platoon of those men than a battalion of regular infantry."

On the night of June 18, the 325th GIR established another bridgehead across the Douve River, with Companies E and G, 325th GIR, crossing in assault boats at Pont-l'Abbé and capturing the village of La Quenauderie on the south side. Once again, the bridge over the causeway was repaired, and the remainder of the 325th GIR crossed on foot and pushed the bridgehead south and west to the edge of the Bois de Limors.

The 507th PIR attacked west from Cretteville to capture Vindefontaine the following day. The 3rd Battalion, 508th, then moved south through Vindefontaine and attacked Pretot. After cleaning out the town, the battalion was ordered to withdraw to high ground overlooking the town because of massive and accurate German artillery and mortar fire. The 505th PIR attacked through the Bois de Limors and dug in on the western edge later that day.

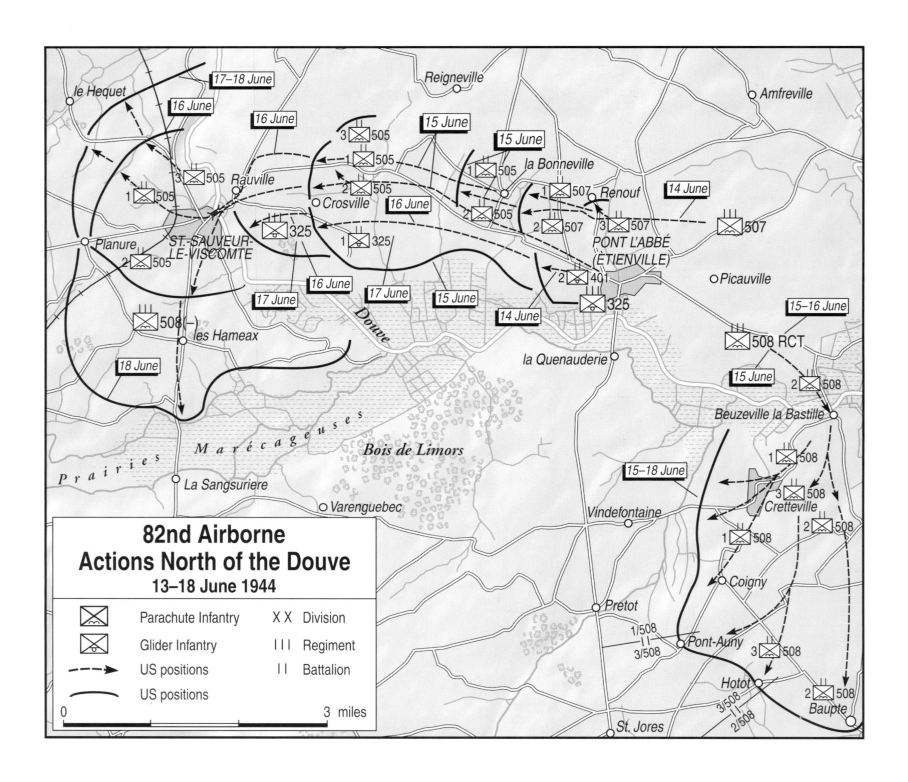

**82nd Airborne
Actions North of the Douve**
13–18 June 1944

🪂 Parachute Infantry	X X Division
🪂 Glider Infantry	I I I Regiment
--➤ US positions	I I Battalion
⟋ US positions	

0   3   miles

le Hequet

Reigneville

Amfreville

17–18 June

16 June

16 June

15 June

15 June

3 ⊠ 505

1 ⊠ 505

2 ⊠ 505

3 ⊠ 505

1 ⊠ 505

Rauville

Crosville

la Bonneville

1 ⊠ 505

14 June

16 June

1 ⊠ 507

Renouf

2 ⊠ 507

2 ⊠ 505

3 ⊠ 507

⊠ 507

2 ⊠ 507

PONT L'ABBÉ
(ÉTIENVILLE)

Planure

ST-SAUVEUR-
LE-VISCOMTE

⊞ 325

1 ⊠ 325

Picauville

2 ⊠ 505

2 ⊠ 401

Douve

16 June

17 June

17 June

15 June

14 June

⊞ 325

⊞ 508 (–)

les Hameax

18 June

15–16 June

⊞ 508 RCT

15 June

2 ⊠ 508

la Quenauderie

Beuzeville la Bastille

Maréc ageuses

Bois de Limors

1 ⊠ 508

Prairies

15–18 June

3 ⊠ 508

Cretteville

La Sangsuriere

Vindefontaine

1 ⊠ 508

2 ⊠ 508

Varenguebec

Coigny

Pretot

1/508
3/508

3 ⊠ 508

Pont-Auny

Hotot

3/508
2/508

2 ⊠ 508

Baupte

St. Jores

A French-made Renault tank captured by the Germans in 1940 and used in Normandy, destroyed by the 80th Airborne Antiaircraft (Antitank) Battalion. Possibly one the five tanks and self-propelled guns knocked out by Staff Sergeant Richard E. Rider near Baupte on June 13, 1944. Rider was later awarded the Distinguished Service Cross for this extraordinary feat of arms. *Photograph by James Baugh, courtesy of Mrs. James Baugh*

General Gavin and Colonel Lewis use a 1:25,000-scale map to discuss the details of the attack toward St.-Sauveur-le-Vicomte, June 14, 1944. *Photographic still of U.S. Army combat camera film, courtesy of Tyler Alberts and www.combatreels.com*

Paratroopers with the 505th PIR move through a Norman town. *Photograph by Dr. Daniel B. McIlvoy, courtesy of Mrs. Ann McIlvoy Zaya*

The devastation of Picauville as elements of the 82nd Airborne Division move through it. *U.S. Army photograph, courtesy of the 82nd Airborne Division War Memorial Museum*

Major Whitfield Jack, the division's G-2 (Assistant Chief of Staff, Intelligence), shakes hands with a French informant, who has provided information about German dispositions. *U.S. Army photograph, courtesy of the 82nd Airborne Division War Memorial Museum*

German wounded await treatment, while their dead comrades lie in the ditch on the right side of the photo. *Photograph courtesy of the 82nd Airborne Division War Memorial Museum*

A machine gun crew with the 325th GIR sets up in an opening of a hedgerow. *U.S. Army photograph, courtesy of the 82nd Airborne Division War Memorial Museum*

One of two German 75mm antitank guns that opposed Company D, 505th PIR, at Rosiers, east of St.-Sauveur-le-Vicomte, June 15, 1944. *Photograph by Dr. Daniel B. McIlvoy, courtesy of Mrs. Ann McIlvoy Zaya*

A German self-propelled gun mounting a high-velocity 75mm gun, knocked out in the fighting east of St.-Sauveur-le-Vicomte. *U.S. Army photograph, courtesy of the 82nd Airborne Division War Memorial Museum*

A paratrooper holding a camera looks through a German self-propelled gun, apparently abandoned, with ammunition and no visible signs of destruction to the gun platform. *U.S. Army photograph, courtesy of the 82nd Airborne Division War Memorial Museum*

This aerial photograph of St.-Sauveur-le-Vicomte looks west, with the Douve River in the lower portion. Note the shell holes and bomb craters near the river. When the 505th PIR crossed the river at a damaged bridge (lower right) under enemy fire on June 16, 1944, they had outrun the bomb line and were attacked by Allied fighter-bombers. The bridge had been repaired, but the damage to the buildings along the main road remained at the time of this photograph. *U.S. Army photograph, courtesy of the National Archives*

Troopers with the 325th GIR test a captured German Panzerschreck, a powerful antitank weapon. *U.S. Army photograph, courtesy of the 82nd Airborne Division War Memorial Museum*

Paratroopers of the 82nd Airborne Division and a detachment of the 307th Airborne Medical Company move through a Norman town. *U.S. Army photograph, courtesy of the 82nd Airborne Division War Memorial Museum*

A second aerial photograph of St.-Sauveur-le-Vicomte. *U.S. Army photograph, courtesy of the National Archives*

Chapter 18

"RESOURCEFUL AND COURAGEOUS IN THE ATTACK, RESOLUTE IN THE DEFENSE, THEY FOUGHT SUPERBLY"

The division consolidated its bridgehead south of Douve River on June 21, 1944. The division held a line from the western and southern edge of the Bois de Limors southeasterly to Pretot. The worst storm in fifty years hit the English Channel and Normandy from June 19 to 21. The Germans used the respite to fortify their positions lay minefields and booby traps in the front of them, and pre-register artillery and mortars. Lieutenant Stanley Weinberg, with Company B, 505th PIR, led three deep-penetration patrols during this period that gained valuable information about German dispositions.

On July 3, the division attacked southwesterly toward La Haye-du-Puits, with the 505th PIR on the right attacking the northern slope and crest of Hill 131, the 508th PIR in the center attacking toward the southern slope of Hill 131, and the 325th GIR on the left attacking toward Hill 95. The 507th PIR screened the left rear of the division attack.

Using the intelligence from the Weinberg patrols, the 505th PIR took a flank route to the rear of the German main line of resistance and struck it from behind. The regiment moved up the northern slope of Hill 131 and cut the highway from La Haye-du-Puits to St.-Sauveur-le-

Vicomte. The 508th PIR ran into heavy enemy opposition but reached the southern slope of Hill 131.

The 325th GIR on the left attacked toward Hill 95, but encountered heavy German counterattacks on its left flank from the La Poterie Ridge in the U.S. 90th Infantry Division's sector. That afternoon the objectives were changed, and the 325th GIR attacked toward the eastern end of the La Poterie ridgeline and the town of La Poterie, while the 508th PIR attacked toward Hill 95, and the 505th PIR captured the southern slope of Hill 131. By nightfall, Hill 131 was secure, while the 508th PIR had dug in at the foot of Hill 95. The 325th GIR had fought hard on the eastern end of the La Poterie ridgeline, almost reaching the town of La Poterie.

The following morning, the 505th PIR attacked through the depleted 508th PIR and seized the northern slope of Hill 95. The 2nd Battalion, 508th PIR, moved through the 505th PIR line and fought until midnight to capture the crest of Hill 95. The remainder of the 508th PIR attacked the center and eastern hills of the La Poterie ridgeline. The 325th GIR continued to meet very tough opposition as it slugged its way toward the town of La Poterie from the northeast. That night, the 507th PIR captured the highest hill in the center and the northern slopes of the eastern hill mass of the ridgeline.

On the morning of July 5, 1944, the 325th GIR finally captured the town of La Poterie. On July 8, the division was placed in corps reserve and moved back a couple of miles and assembled. On July 11, the division moved to Utah Beach and loaded on to seventeen LSTs for the trip back to England.

General Gavin felt that the accolades for the victory in Normandy belonged to the enlisted men, noncommissioned officers, and officers who had sacrificed so much: "The troopers had been splendid; resourceful and courageous in the attack, resolute in the defense, they fought superbly."

A machine gun crew with the 325th GIR aims through a gate along a hedgerow in Normandy. *U.S. Army photograph, courtesy of the 82nd Airborne Division War Memorial Museum*

Lieutenant Stanley Weinberg, a platoon leader with Company B, 505th PIR, talks over his walkie-talkie radio while holding his 1928 model Thompson submachine gun with the wooden pistol grip under the barrel. *Photograph courtesy of Ann Weinberg*

A .30-caliber air-cooled machine gun manned by a trooper with the 325th GIR. *U.S. Army photograph, courtesy of the 82nd Airborne Division War Memorial Museum*

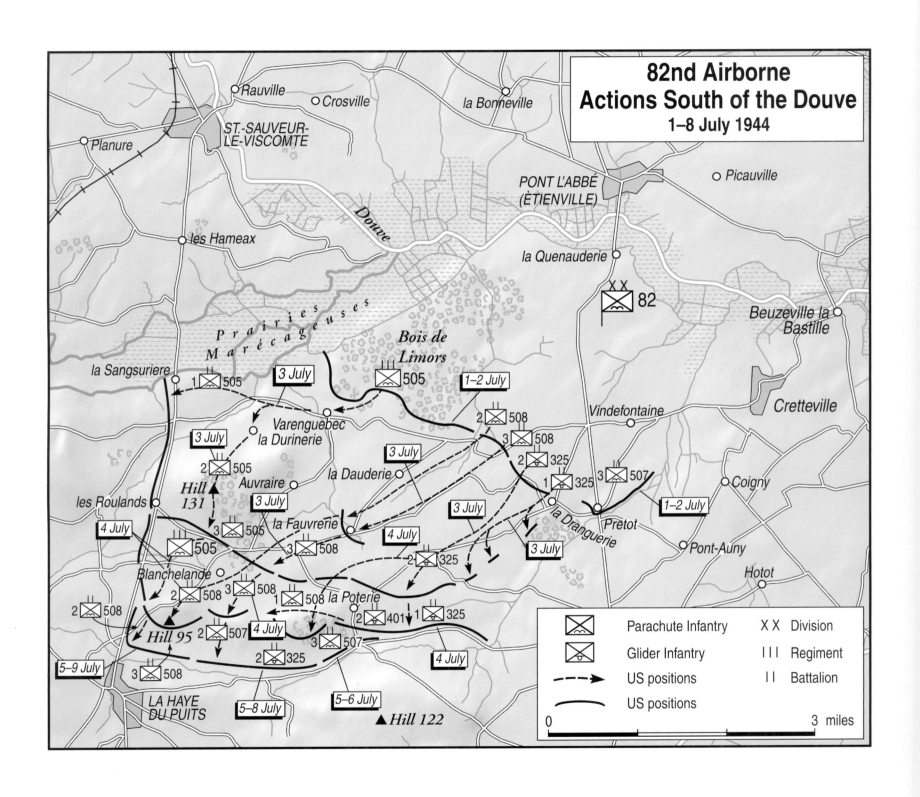

**82nd Airborne
Actions South of the Douve**
1–8 July 1944

Rauville

Crosville

la Bonneville

ST.-SAUVEUR-
LE-VISCOMTE

Planure

PONT L'ABBÉ
(ÈTIENVILLE)

Picauville

les Hameax

Douve

la Quenauderie

XX 82

Beuzeville la
Bastille

Prairies
Marécageuses

Bois de
Limors

Cretteville

la Sangsuriere

1 ⊠ 505

3 July

⊠ 505

1–2 July

Vindefontaine

Varenguebec
la Durinerie

2 ⊠ 508

3 July

2 ⊠ 505

3 July

Auvraire

la Dauderie

3 ⊠ 508

2 ⊠ 325

Coigny

1 ⊠ 325

3 ⊠ 507

les Roulands

Hill
131

3 July

3 ⊠ 505

la Fauvrerie

3 ⊠ 508

4 July

2 ⊠ 325

3 July

la Dranguerie

Pretot

1–2 July

4 July

⊠ 505

3 July

Pont-Auny

Blanchelande

2 ⊠ 508

3 ⊠ 508

1 ⊠ 508

la Poterie

Hotot

2 ⊠ 508

2 ⊠ 401

1 ⊠ 325

Hill 95

2 ⊠ 507

4 July

3 ⊠ 507

2 ⊠ 325

4 July

5–9 July

3 ⊠ 508

LA HAYE
DU PUITS

5–8 July

5–6 July

▲ Hill 122

⊠ Parachute Infantry	X X	Division
⊠ Glider Infantry	I I I	Regiment
- - -▶ US positions	I I	Battalion
⌒ US positions		

0 _____ 3 miles

Left to right: Private First Class Alphonse A. Caplick, Staff Sergeant Harold J. Brogan, Corporal Robert L. Stutt, and Private First Class Michael (Nikaluski) Nichols, all with Company B, 508th PIR. On July 4, 1944, Caplick and Nichols would be wounded and Brogan and Stutt would be killed in action during fighting on the La Poterie ridgeline. *Photograph courtesy of Bill Call*

General Omar Bradley pins the Distinguished Service Cross (DSC) on Lieutenant Colonel Benjamin H. Vandervoort. Captain Robert D. Rae, who led the composite company of the 507th PIR during the attack across the La Fière Causeway on June 9, 1944, stands at attention to the left of Vandervoort to receive the DSC. *U.S. Army photograph, courtesy of the 82nd Airborne Division War Memorial Museum*

A second view of the ceremony, left to right: Brigadier General James M. Gavin, Lieutenant Colonel Edward C. Krause, Lieutenant Colonel Benjamin H. Vandervoort, and Captain Robert D. Rae are awarded the Distinguished Service Cross or the Oak Leaf to the DSC for extraordinary heroism during the capture and defense of Ste.-Mère-Église and the attack to capture the La Fière Causeway. *U.S. Army photograph, courtesy of the 82nd Airborne Division War Memorial Museum*

Lieutenant Stanley Weinberg stands behind the truck that holds what remains of his Company B, 505th PIR, platoon at the end of the Normandy campaign. *Photograph courtesy of Ann Weinberg*

The temporary cemetery at Blosville that held the dead of the 82nd Airborne Division killed in Normandy. The division suffered 1,142 killed or dead of wounds, 2,373 wounded, and 840 captured or missing out of 11,770 officers and men: a forty-six percent casualty rate. *U.S. Army photograph, courtesy of the 82nd Airborne Division War Memorial Museum*

Landing ships tank (LSTs) at Utah Beach waiting to load the division for the trip across the Channel to England, July 11, 1944. *Photograph courtesy of Ann Weinberg*

Lieutenant Stanley Weinberg, with Company B, 505th PIR, took this photograph of the troopers of the 505th PIR loading on an LST at Utah Beach, July 11, 1944. *Photograph courtesy of Ann Weinberg*

Sergeant Robert D. Henderson (center) and Sergeant Harvill W. Lazenby (right), both with Company B, 505th PIR, are given food by Private John C. Rodrigues. Henderson and Lazenby were captured on June 6, 1944, but escaped several days later during a night march. They lived on raw potatoes and traveled at night to make their way back to American lines on July 16, 1944. *U.S. Army photograph, courtesy of the 82nd Airborne Division War Memorial Museum*

Chapter 19

"PUT US DOWN IN HOLLAND, OR PUT US DOWN IN HELL, BUT PUT US DOWN ALL IN ONE PLACE OR I WILL HOUND YOU TO YOUR GRAVES!"

After the return to England, the division received replacements and some of the wounded returned from the hospitals to fill the ranks and bring the division back to full strength. The 507th PIR, which had suffered the highest casualty rate of the division's four regiments in Normandy, was transferred to the newly forming 17th Airborne Division to make room for the 504th PIR.

On August 16, 1944, General Gavin assumed command of the division after General Ridgway was promoted to command the newly formed XVIII Airborne Corps. Gavin immediately put a new staff together; most of the division's staff had gone with Ridgway to the XVIII Airborne Corps.

In mid-August the Allies broke out of the Normandy lodgment and pursued the remnants of the German Army across France and into Belgium. Two airborne operations planned for early September to seize key bridges in Belgium were cancelled, as Allied armor overran the areas.

But, on September 10, General Gavin was briefed on a plan for a massive airborne operation involving the 82nd, 101st, and British 1st Airborne divisions. They were to seize key bridges in Holland to facilitate a drive by the British Second Army across the Rhine River and into the industrial Ruhr Valley of Germany. The operation, code named Market-Garden, was ordered to commence on September 17.

General Gavin's new G-3 (operations section) staff officer, Lieutenant Colonel Jack Norton, and his staff put together a detailed plan for the division in only three days—a truly remarkable feat. The plan called for the division to drop fifty-three miles behind German lines. The 504th PIR was assigned to capture the Grave bridge over the Maas River and the bridges over the Maas-Waal Canal. The 505th PIR was ordered to seize the town of Groesbeek and the heights south of Nijmegen, and defend against an attack from the Reichswald. The 508th PIR was to take the high ground east of Nijmegen and once secured, capture the Nijmegen highway bridge over the Waal River.

The 307th Engineer Battalion, the 376th PFA Battalion, and Battery A, 80th Antiaircraft Battalion, would support the three parachute infantry regiments until the following day, when the division's artillery and antitank forces would land by glider. The 325th GIR would be brought in by glider with the third lift.

Preparations moved at a frantic pace, and by September 16 the parachute elements were at the airfields and ready to go. At a joint briefing for his battalion and their troop-carrier crews, Lieutenant Neal Beaver, with Company H, 508th, listened to the air corps and then the weatherman.

Next came our battalion commander, Lieutenant Colonel Louis G. Mendez Jr. The room was noisy and stuffy and hot. Colonel Mendez stood before that group of his own officers and the pilots and said not a word for at least two or three minutes.

Then in the dead hush he had created he said, "Gentlemen, my officers know this map by heart—and we are ready to go."

"When I brought my battalion to the briefing prior to Normandy, I had the finest combat-ready force of its size that will ever be known! Gentlemen, by the time I had gathered them together in Normandy—one half of them were gone!" (Tears were rolling down his cheeks at this point.)

"I charge you all—put us down in Holland, or put us down in Hell, but put us down All In One Place or I will hound you to your graves!"

He turned and walked out.

General Gavin's jeep is backed into the nose of the CG-4A Waco glider that will transport it to Holland the following day, September 17, 1944. *U.S. Army photograph courtesy of the Cornelius Ryan Collection, Alden Library, Ohio University*

Paratroopers enjoy a meal that is a combination fried chicken dinner and breakfast, September 17, 1944. *U.S. Army photograph, courtesy of the Cornelius Ryan Collection, Alden Library, Ohio University*

Paratroopers gather around a map to review their assignments, September 17, 1944. *Photograph courtesy of Jerome V. Huth*

Paratroopers with the 508th PIR carry equipment bundles to their aircraft in the early morning hours of September 17, 1944. *U.S. Army photograph, courtesy of the 82nd Airborne Division War Memorial Museum*

Materials used to make Gammon grenades are issued, September 17, 1944. *U.S. Army photograph, courtesy of the 82nd Airborne Division War Memorial Museum*

Scale maps of Groesbeek (1:25,000) and Hertogenbosch (1:100,000) are issued to the troopers, September 17, 1944. *U.S. Army photograph, courtesy of the Cornelius Ryan Collection, Alden Library, Ohio University*

General Gavin chutes up for the Holland jump, September 17, 1944. *U.S. Army photograph, courtesy of the 82nd Airborne Division War Memorial Museum*

An officer refers to a map while giving his men a last-minute briefing, September 17, 1944. *U.S. Army photograph, courtesy of the 82nd Airborne Division War Memorial Museum*

General Gavin, with his parachute, reserve chute, musette bag, and assembled M1 rifle, just before boarding his plane, September 17, 1944. *U.S. Army photograph, courtesy of the 82nd Airborne Division War Memorial Museum*

Paratroopers with Company H, 505th PIR pose for a photo before boarding their aircraft, September 17, 1944. *Photograph courtesy of Weldon Grissom*

Members of Lieutenant Stanley Weinberg's stick of Company B, 505th PIR, pose for a photo prior to boarding their C-47, September 17, 1944. *Photograph courtesy of Ann Weinberg*

A paratrooper struggles with his heavy load to climb the steps of the airplane, September 17, 1944. *U.S. Army photograph, courtesy of the 82nd Airborne Division War Memorial Museum*

A stick of paratroopers loaded down with parachutes, weapons, and equipment board their plane, September 17, 1944. *Photograph by Daniel B. McIlvoy, courtesy of Ann McIlvoy Zaya*

Troopers with Company H, 505th PIR, wait in line to board their plane, September 17, 1944. *Photograph courtesy of Weldon Grissom*

A stick of paratroopers await takeoff for Holland, September 17, 1944. *U.S. Army photograph, courtesy of the 82nd Airborne Division War Memorial Museum*

General Gavin's stick is ready for takeoff. Lieutenant Colonel Jack Norton is seated on the left, September 17, 1944. *U.S. Army photograph, courtesy of the 82nd Airborne Division War Memorial Museum*

Chapter 20

"THIS MIGHTY SPECTACLE DEEPLY IMPRESSED ME"

At 10:19 a.m. on September 17, 1944, C-47s carrying paratroopers of the 82nd Airborne Division began lifting off the runways from six airfields in England at five-second intervals, climbing to altitude, and vectoring to form up into the serial formations. As the troop-carrier aircraft carrying the division's paratroopers joined the one-hundred-mile-long sky train carrying elements of three airborne divisions, Allied fighter planes appeared above and on the flanks to suppress any enemy antiaircraft or fighter-plane opposition.

German General Kurt Student, commander of all German parachute forces, watched the gigantic force sweep over the positions of his troops in front of the British Second Army. "This mighty spectacle deeply impressed me. I thought with reflection and longing of our own airborne operations, and I said [to his chief of staff, Colonel] Reinhard, 'Oh if ever I'd had such means at my disposal. Just once, to have this many planes.'"

With the 505th PIR in the lead, followed by the 504th PIR, the 508th PIR, and finally fifty gliders carrying Battery A, 80th Antiaircraft (Antitank) Battalion and headquarters personnel, the serials of C-47s and their fighter escorts flew over the coast of Holland, flooded by the Germans to prevent amphibious landings. Enemy antiaircraft guns began firing at the C-47s overhead, and Allied fighters dived to strafe, bomb, and fire rockets at those guns.

Enemy flak increased as the division's serials approached the drop zones. Because of a slight timing problem, the serial carrying Lieutenant Colonel Vandervoort's 2nd Battalion, 505th PIR, arrived near the 505th PIR's Drop Zone "N," southeast of Groesbeek, just as Major James L. Kaiser's 3rd Battalion, 505th PIR, serial approached. Vandervoort quickly made the decision to divert his battalion to the open ground northeast of Groesbeek, a short distance away. The 505th PIR, except for the 2nd Battalion, landed on the drop zone with only the loss of two aircraft.

The 504th PIR jumped minutes later just north of the Maas River on Drop Zone "O," near Over Asselt, except for Company E, which dropped just south of the river near the Grave Bridge so that the bridge could be assaulted from both ends. Only two aircraft were lost during the flight and jump.

Companies B, C, and D, 307th Airborne Engineer Battalion, jumped on Drop Zone "N" four minutes later and did not lose an aircraft to enemy fire. The 508th PIR jumped a few minutes afterward on Drop Zone "T," northeast of Groesbeek, and encountered the most intense antiaircraft fire on the flight to their drop zone, resulting in the loss of six aircraft.

The last parachute element to arrive was the 376th Parachute Field Artillery Battalion, on Drop Zone "N," just twenty minutes after the three engineer companies. No planes were lost with this serial. The serial of fifty gliders landed on Landing Zone "N," without the loss of a plane or glider to enemy antiaircraft fire. The paratroopers immediately assembled and began moving to their assigned initial objectives.

Next page: The parachutes of Companies B, C, and D, 307th Airborne Engineer Battalion, over Drop Zone "N," September 17, 1944. *Photograph by Stanley Weinberg, courtesy of Ann Weinberg*

The serial carrying the 1st Battalion, 504th PIR, passes over the flooded area on the coast of Holland, September 17, 1944. *U.S. Army Air Corps photograph*

The aircraft in this photo have tightened their formation and descended to the proper altitude in preparation for the jump. *U.S. Army photograph, courtesy of the 82nd Airborne Division War Memorial Museum*

A paratrooper with the 3rd Battalion, 505th PIR, exits the door of his C-47 over Drop Zone "N," southeast of Groesbeek, Holland, September 17, 1944. *U.S. Army Air Corps photograph*

The 1st Battalion, 505th, drops on Drop Zone "N," near Groesbeek, Holland, September 17, 1944. *U.S. Army Air Corps photograph*

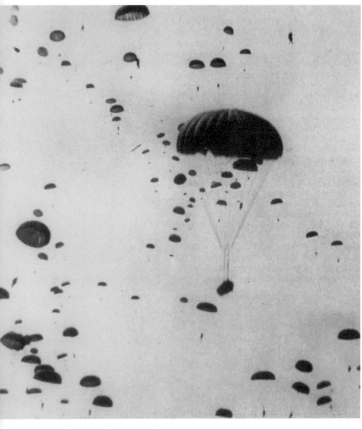

The 505th PIR mass jump over Drop Zone "N." The view is toward the south, with the Maas River in the lower portion of the photo running from left to right. *Photographic still of U.S. Army combat film, courtesy of the National Archives*

A parachute with an equipment bundle can be seen in the right center of the photograph amid the parachutes of the 1st Battalion, 505th PIR, September 17, 1944. *Photographic still of U.S. Army combat film, courtesy of the National Archives*

Paratroopers with the 505th PIR land on Drop Zone "N," September 17, 1944. *Photographic still of U.S. Army combat film, courtesy of the National Archives*

The assembly of the 1st Battalion, 505th PIR, on Drop Zone "N," September 17, 1944. *Photograph by Stanley Weinberg, courtesy of Ann Weinberg*

The 504th PIR jumps on Drop Zone "O," just north of the Maas River, near Over Asselt, Holland, September 17, 1944. *U.S. Army Air Corps photograph*

The 376th Parachute Field Artillery Battalion drop on Drop Zone "N," twenty minutes after the three engineer companies, September 17, 1944. *Photograph by Stanley Weinberg courtesy of Ann Weinberg*

Chapter 21

"SITUATION WELL IN HAND"

Upon landing, all three parachute regiments immediately moved to seize their objectives. The most important of those initial objectives was the Grave Bridge, the longest bridge in Europe. If the Germans blew the bridge before it could be taken, the British ground forces would have a huge task to build a bridge across the wide Maas River before any link-up could take place with the 82nd Airborne Division. Company E, 504th PIR, landed south of the bridge and advanced toward the southern approach while taking fire from a 20mm antiaircraft gun mounted on a flak tower near the southern end of the bridge and from Germans in the town of Grave. The rest of the 2nd Battalion, 504th PIR, moved west from the drop zone near Over Asselt and attacked the northern approach of the bridge. German 20mm antiaircraft guns on a tower on the northern bridge approach and positioned between the riverbanks and the dikes, as well as machine gun nests, were overrun as the troopers closed on the bridge. Both ends were captured quickly and the bridge secured. The 2nd Battalion troopers moved across to join Company E in attacking and cleaning out the town of Grave and establishing a block to the south on the road to the bridge.

The 1st Battalion, 504th PIR, attacked the Heumen lock bridge (Bridge 7) and the bridge at Blankenberg (Bridge 8) that crossed the Maas-Waal Canal. Bridge 8 was blown just as the troopers with Company C reached the approach. Company B attacked and captured the critical bridge at Heumen in a battle that lasted into the night. Corporal Charles

Nau and Sergeant Shelton Dustin were each awarded the Distinguished Service Cross for extraordinary acts of valor during the attack.

In the 505th PIR sector, the 2nd Battalion moved east from Drop Zone "T" through Groesbeek, helping the 3rd Battalion clean out the town against little opposition, then seized the high ground west of the town. Company I established blocks on the roads leading out of the Reichswald to Groesbeek. After clearing Groesbeek, the 3rd Battalion established a perimeter east and south of Groesbeek facing the Reichswald. The 1st Battalion seized the towns of Mook, Riethorst, and Plasmolen against light opposition and established blocks on the road connecting the towns. Company B attempted to seize the railroad bridge over the Maas River just west of Mook, but it was blown as they approached.

The 2nd Battalion, 508th PIR, secured Drop Zone "T" and established a perimeter northeast of Groesbeek. The 3rd Battalion captured the high ground east of Nijmegen against little opposition. The 1st Battalion moved to block the road south from Nijmegen and then after dark moved into Nijmegen to capture the highway bridge, but ran into stiff German opposition with the arrival of the 9th SS Reconnaissance Battalion from the Arnhem area. The battalion was stopped short of the bridge in fierce house-to-house and street fighting.

With the Nijmegen bridges the only major objectives remaining, the three parachute regiments reported to General Gavin that they had the "situation well in hand."

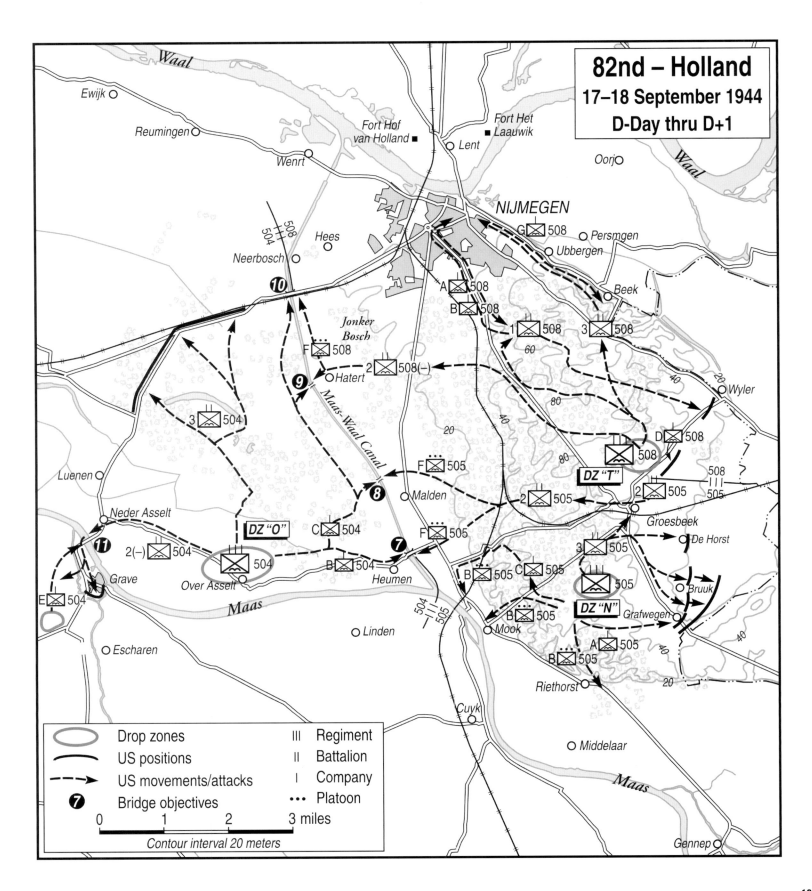

82nd – Holland
17–18 September 1944
D-Day thru D+1

Waal

Ewijk

Reumingen

Wenrt

Fort Hof
van Holland ■

Lent

Fort Het
Laauwik ■

Oorjo

Waal

NIJMEGEN

G 508   Persmgen

Ubbergen

Hees

Neerbosch

508
504

10

Jonker
Bosch

F 508

9

2 508(–)

Hatert

Maas-Waal Canal

A 508
B 508

1 508   3 508

60

40

20

Beek

40

Wyler

508

3 504

20

80

80

D 508

DZ "T"

2 505   508
III
505

Luenen

8

F 505

Malden

2 505

Groesbeek

Neder Asselt

11

2(–) 504

DZ "O"

C 504

B 504

504

Over Asselt

7

F 505

Heumen

B 505   C 505

3 505   De Horst

505

DZ "N"   Grafwegen

Bruuk

Grave

E 504

Maas

Linden

504
III
505

B 505

Mook

A 505

B 505

40

20

Escharen

Riethorst

Cuyk

Middelaar

Maas

Gennep

<table>
<tr><td>⬭</td><td>Drop zones</td><td>III</td><td>Regiment</td></tr>
<tr><td>⌒</td><td>US positions</td><td>II</td><td>Battalion</td></tr>
<tr><td>- - -▶</td><td>US movements/attacks</td><td>I</td><td>Company</td></tr>
<tr><td>❼</td><td>Bridge objectives</td><td>• • •</td><td>Platoon</td></tr>
</table>

0   1   2   3 miles

Contour interval 20 meters

An aerial view facing north of the Grave Bridge over the Maas River and the ancient town of Grave, with its old walled fortifications. The concrete pillbox and flak tower guarding the southern approach can be seen along the left side of the road as it curves toward the bridge. *Photograph by 541 Squadron, RAF, courtesy of Frits Janssen*

The Grave Bridge, the longest bridge in Europe at that time. Troopers of the 2nd Battalion, 504th PIR, charged across the bridge under fire from German 20mm antiaircraft guns firing from the ground between the river and the dikes. *Photograph courtesy of the Cornelius Ryan Collection, Alden Library, Ohio University*

A view of the Heumen lock bridge, captured intact by Company B, 504th PIR, after a fight that lasted into the night of September 17–18. *Photograph courtesy of the Cornelius Ryan Collection, Alden Library, Ohio University*

An aerial view of the Heumen lock bridge, code-named Bridge 7, across the Maas-Waal Canal. *U.S. Army photograph, courtesy of the Cornelius Ryan Collection, Alden Library, Ohio University*

Troopers with the Regimental Headquarters and the 2nd Battalion, 505th PIR, move toward Kamp on the way to the assembly point at the observatory at Molenberg, just north of Groesbeek, September 17, 1944. *Photograph by William Jenks*

The assembly point for the 2nd Battalion, 505th PIR, was this observatory, converted to a flak tower by the Germans. Vandervoort's veterans made short work of eliminating enemy flak guns on the drop zone, September 17, 1944. *Photograph courtesy of the 82nd Airborne Division War Memorial Museum*

Troopers have stopped these two cars and are searching a German soldier with his hands over his head in the center of the photo, near the observatory on the northern edge of Groesbeek, September 17, 1944. *Photograph by William Jenks*

Colonel William E. Ekman, commander of the 505th PIR (facing the camera) confers with his staff near the car and the captured German, September 17, 1944. *Photograph by William Jenks*

Paratroopers with the Regimental Headquarters Company, 505th PIR, move down the main street in Groesbeek, September 17, 1944. *Photograph courtesy of Jerome V. Huth*

Captain Harold E. Miller, commander of Company B, 505th PIR (left) and his executive officer, Lieutenant James Irvin (center) on Drop Zone "N," September 17, 1944. *Photograph by Stanley Weinberg, courtesy of Ann Weinberg*

Lieutenant Stanley Weinberg's Company B, 505th, platoon shot up this Opel staff car heading on the Nijmegen-to-Gennep highway east of Mook, near Plasmolen, killing a German lieutenant colonel and capturing the driver and a major. *Photograph by Stanley Weinberg, courtesy of Ann Weinberg*

An aerial view of the railroad bridge at Molenhoek over the Maas River that was blown by Germans on September 17, 1944, as Company B, 505th PIR, approached from the north. *Photograph by 541 Squadron, RAF, courtesy of Frits Janssen*

Brigadier General Gavin (center) and Major William H. Johnson, 307th Airborne Engineer Battalion (right), talk on the drop zone before moving to the site planned for the division command post, as Lieutenant Colonel Alfred Ireland, division G-1 (left), listens. *U.S. Army photograph, courtesy of the 82nd Airborne Division War Memorial Museum*

Captain Hugo Olson, General Gavin's aide, holding a map in front of tree marked "Champion Message Center" in white chalk, September 17, 1944. *U.S. Army photograph, courtesy of the 82nd Airborne Division War Memorial Museum*

At the divisional command post, General Gavin (left) returns a salute as Dutch liaison officer Captain Arie D. Bestebreurtje (second from right) discusses taking out the German machine gun crew. *U.S. Army photograph, courtesy of the 82nd Airborne Division War Memorial Museum*

The "Champion CP" signs points the way to the division command post. *U.S. Army photograph, courtesy of the Cornelius Ryan Collection, Alden Library, Ohio University*

Chapter 22

"WE'VE COME A LONG WAY . . . TELL THE BOYS TO DO A GOOD JOB"

On the morning of September 18, the 508th PIR attacked and captured Bridge 10 over the Maas-Waal Canal after a costly assault. Also that morning, German infantry overran part of Landing Zone "T" northeast of Groesbeek and set up a number of 20mm antiaircraft guns on and around the landing zone to await the inevitable glider reinforcements. Southeast of Groesbeek, German infantry infiltrated on to the Landing Zone "N," in the 505th PIR sector, as a three-company attack hit the 505th PIR perimeter about 8:30 a.m. from the Reichswald.

In England, 454 gliders carrying the balance of the division's artillery and antitank guns began taking off about an hour late due to fog. They would arrive at the two landing zones starting at about 3:00 p.m.

In the 508th PIR sector, every rifle company was committed, so at about 10:00 a.m., Colonel Roy Lindquist, the commander of the 508th PIR, ordered the 1st Battalion to disengage in Nijmegen, march eight miles, and clear Landing Zone "T" before the gliders arrived. The 1st Battalion, 508th PIR, arrived on the northwest side of Landing Zone "T" at about 2:30 p.m. and immediately deployed into skirmish lines and began moving toward the German infantry and antiaircraft guns. The Germans unleashed a storm of machine gun

and 20mm fire. With Company B on the right, Company C on the left, and Company A following, the battalion advanced steadily in the face of the heavy fire and overran the German infantry and attacked the 20mm antiaircraft guns, just as the first gliders began to land. Out in front of Company C, Sergeant Leonard A. Funk was credited with killing twenty and wounding the remainder of the antiaircraft gun crews in the Company C sector. He would later be awarded the Distinguished Service Cross for this action. The 1st Battalion, 508th PIR, cleared the landing zone and knocked out sixteen 20mm antiaircraft guns and their crews.

The gliders landed under fire, with some coming down to the east, near Wyler, Germany, where most of the passengers and pilots made their way to the 508th PIR perimeter. At Landing Zone "N," Company C, 505th PIR, led by Captain Anthony "Stef" Stefanich, attacked and drove the enemy infantry before them as the gliders began to arrive. Most of the gliders landed behind the Company C skirmish line. However, one glider came in over the heads of Stefanich's men, crash-landing near the German positions on the edge of the Reichswald. Hoping to rescue the glider pilot and any passengers, Stefanich yelled for his men to follow him.

As they neared the glider, Lieutenant Gus Sanders ran a few yards in front of the others and was firing a BAR at the fleeing Germans. "Stef yelled for me to get down, and about that time he was hit."

As the medic administered first aid, Sanders, standing over Captain Stefanich, saw him look up. "He only said a few words, 'Gus, we've come a long way . . . tell the boys to do a good job.'" Moments later, Stefanich died.

As the gliders landed on Landing Zone "N," eleven German tanks were spotted moving up to support the infantry that was attacking Company I, 505th PIR. The 376th PFA Battalion hit the tanks with pinpoint accuracy, knocking out five and forcing the others back to the Reichswald. Then, Company I counterattacked and drove the German infantry back into the Reichswald.

The next morning, the British Guards Armoured Division linked up with the 82nd Airborne Division.

Two Waco gliders over Holland, carrying troopers of the 82nd Airborne Division, September 18, 1944. *U.S. Army photograph, courtesy of the 82nd Airborne Division War Memorial Museum*

General Gavin looks over a map as he
assesses the situation on the morning of
September 18, 1944. *U.S. Army photograph,
courtesy of the 82nd Airborne Division War
Memorial Museum*

General Gavin (left) meets with Lieutenant Colonel Shields
Warren, commander of the 1st Battalion, 508th PIR (right), to
discuss the attack by his battalion to clear Landing Zone "T,"
northeast of Groesbeek, Holland, September 18, 1944. *U.S.
Army photograph, courtesy of the 82nd Airborne Division War
Memorial Museum*

Aerial view of Landing Zone "T," with gliders and empty
parachutes scattered over the area. *Photograph courtesy of the
82nd Airborne Division War Memorial Museum*

A CG-4A glider explodes at Landing Zone "N," September 18, 1944. *Photographic still of U.S. Army combat film, courtesy of the 82nd Airborne Division War Memorial Museum*

A second photo of gliders on Landing Zone "N," September 18, 1944. *Photograph courtesy of the Silent Wings Museum*

Empty gliders sit on the soft farm fields after landing on Landing Zone "N." *Photograph courtesy of the Silent Wings Museum*

Another photo of the gliders on Landing Zone "N," September 18, 1944. *Photograph by Daniel B. McIlvoy, courtesy of Mrs. Ann McIlvoy Zaya*

This heavily damaged glider was the exception; most landed with little damage. *U.S. Army photograph courtesy of the Cornelius Ryan Collection, Alden Library, Ohio University*

An aerial view of Landing Zone "N" southeast of Groesbeek, Holland. *Photograph by 541 Squadron, RAF, courtesy of Frits Janssen*

The 376th Parachute Field Artillery Battalion broke up an attack by eleven enemy tanks as gliders landed on Landing Zone "N," September 18, 1944. *Photograph by 541 Squadron, RAF, courtesy of Frits Janssen*

Battery A, 320th Glider Field Artillery Battalion, landed on Landing Zone "T" and set up their gun on September 18, 1944. *Photograph courtesy of the Silent Wings Museum*

Aerial resupply of the 82nd Airborne Division by B-24 bombers of the U.S. Eighth Air Force. *U.S. Army Air Corps photograph, courtesy of the National Archives*

Chapter 23

"THE NIJMEGEN BRIDGE MUST BE TAKEN TODAY; AT THE LATEST, TOMORROW"

With the arrival of the British Guards Armoured Division in the 82nd Airborne Division's zone of operations, a joint force consisting of the 2nd Battalion, 505th PIR, an infantry company of the 1st Grenadier Guards Battalion, and four troops of Firefly Sherman tanks from the 2nd Grenadier Guards Battalion was formed to seize the two Nijmegen bridges. Word had come via the Dutch telephone system from the British 1st Airborne Division around Arnhem that the situation was desperate and British armor was needed as soon as possible.

On the afternoon of September 19, as the joint force moved north into Nijmegen, the Western Force, made up of Company D, 505th PIR, one platoon of British infantry, and one troop of tanks, split from the main force and took a route on the outskirts of the city to the railroad bridge area. The main body, called the Eastern Force and comprising the remainder of the 2nd Battalion, 505th PIR, the remainder of the British infantry company, and three troops of tanks, moved toward the highway bridge as adoring crowds of citizens of Nijmegen turned out to cheer them on.

By the afternoon of the 19th, the highway and railroad bridges were defended by approximately two thousand Germans, including the reconnaissance battalion of the 9th SS Panzer Division, which was dug in around the southern approach to the highway bridge in Hunner Park and the ruins of the medieval Valkhof palace.

The Eastern Force encountered pockets of enemy resistance in the built up-areas of two- and three-story buildings in Nijmegen, but quickly eliminated them and moved to the edge of the open area in front of the bridge, a traffic circle, and Hunner Park. As the first British tank entered this open area, it was hit and knocked out by one or more antitank guns that covered all approaches to the bridge. Two more tanks were quickly damaged. Company E, which was the lead infantry force, took over houses overlooking the traffic circle and from the top floors opened fire on the Germans below. A round from an 88mm anti-aircraft gun through one of the houses forced a halt to the action.

Meanwhile, a platoon of the infantry and one troop of tanks attempted a move to the open area to the right to attack the bridge approach from the east, but were stopped as well. Company F, two platoons of British infantry, and another troop of tanks moved west and tried an approach toward Hunner Park from the southwest, but the 88mm antiaircraft gun at the traffic circle caused the British armor to abandon the attack as darkness was setting in.

At the railroad bridge area, the Western Force approached the railroad station and yard south of the bridge from the southwest. Between 750 and 1,000 Germans defended the approach. Two of the five British tanks were knocked out, and enemy machine gun fire stopped an attempt to cross the railroad tracks. It was here that Lieutenant Waverly Wray was killed while leading a squad of Company D troopers. The force pulled back and took over several houses and a church to await another opportunity the following morning.

As darkness approached, General Gavin decided on a daring plan to capture the two bridges the following morning. "Earlier [commander of the British I Airborne Corps, General Frederick E.] Browning had warned me, 'The Nijmegen bridge must be taken today. At the latest, tomorrow.' The capture of the Nijmegen bridge was squarely on my shoulders. This I knew. But most important to me were the lives of General [Robert F.] Urquhart and the British First Airborne."

British armor arrives at Heumen on the morning of September 19, 1944. *U.S. Army photograph, courtesy of the Cornelius Ryan Collection, Alden Library, Ohio University*

General Frederick Browning, commander of the British I Airborne Corps (left), to which the 82nd Airborne Division was attached for Operation Market-Garden, meets with General Gavin (right) at Over Asselt to await the arrival of the British Guards Armored Division, September 19, 1944. *U.S. Army photograph, courtesy of the Cornelius Ryan Collection, Alden Library, Ohio University*

Lieutenant Colonel Vandervoort, commander of the 2nd Battalion, 505th PIR (holding map) and Colonel William E. Ekman, commander of the 505th PIR (second from right), confer with Lieutenant Colonel Edward H. Goulburn, commander of the 1st Grenadier Guards and overall commander of the combined force, in his scout car on Groesbeekseweg as the force moves into Nijmegen, September 19, 1944. *U.S. Army photograph, courtesy of the Cornelius Ryan Collection, Alden Library, Ohio University*

Aerial photo of the Nijmegen bridge areas, taken by 541 Squadron of the RAF on September 19, 1944. The view is facing north, with the railroad bridge on the left and the highway bridge on the right. *Photograph courtesy of Frits Janssen*

An aerial photo with a closer view of the highway bridge area, taken by British 541 Squadron on September 19, 1944. *Photograph courtesy of Frits Janssen*

Citizens greet paratroopers of the 2nd Battalion, 505th PIR, as they move through the outskirts of Nijmegen, September 19, 1944. *Photograph courtesy of the Cornelius Ryan Collection, Alden Library, Ohio University*

The main body of the Eastern Force column is stopped by fire coming from the traffic circle through the open area of the Mariaplein plaza, effectively separating it from the lead elements, September 19, 1944. *Photograph courtesy of the Cornelius Ryan Collection, Alden Library, Ohio University*

One of four British Firefly Sherman tanks at the head of the Eastern Force column on Dr. Claes Noorduynstraat, Nijmegen, points the main gun down Regentessestraat, to protect the left flank, September 19, 1944. *U.S. Army photograph, courtesy of the Cornelius Ryan Collection, Alden Library, Ohio University*

The lead elements of the Eastern Force—one troop of tanks, one section of weapons carriers, one platoon of British infantry in half-tracks, and one platoon of Company E, 505th PIR, paratroopers—made it across the Mariaplein plaza. The vehicles photographed here are waiting for three Sherman tanks to move into the open area around the traffic circle, September 19, 1944. *Photograph courtesy of the Cornelius Ryan Collection, Alden Library, Ohio University*

The lead Grenadier Guards Sherman tank is photographed moments after being hit by German antitank fire, as it moved into the open area near the traffic circle. The tank "brewed up" as the gasoline and ammunition exploded. The troop leader was killed. Two other tanks tried to move into the area just after this photo was taken, and both were damaged by antitank fire as well. *U.S. Army photograph, courtesy of the Cornelius Ryan Collection, Alden Library, Ohio University*

The same tank pictured later at the location where it was knocked out. *U.S. Army photograph, courtesy of the Cornelius Ryan Collection, Alden Library, Ohio University*

Chapter 24

"A DAY UNPRECEDENTED IN THE DIVISION'S COMBAT HISTORY"

During the night of September 19–20, General Gavin held a meeting at his Champion CP with British Generals Browning and Brian G. Horrocks, (commander of the British XXX Corps), senior officers of the Guards Armoured Division, the 82nd Airborne Division staff, and Colonel Reuben Tucker, commander of the 504th PIR. Gavin laid out a bold plan to capture the two Nijmegen bridges. The 504th PIR would execute a daring crossing of the Waal River if sufficient boats could be found, and would conduct an assault to seize the north ends of the two bridges, while the Grenadier Guards and the 2nd Battalion, 505th PIR, simultaneously attacked the southern approaches. The British would supply the boats, but they were positioned somewhere south in the long column of vehicles using the one road north from Eindhoven.

The following morning, four German kampfgruppes made concentric attacks on the division's perimeter. One attacked Wyler with the goal of relieving the defenders in Nijmegen. A second attacked Beek with the same objective. The third came out of the Reichswald, attacking west toward Groesbeek, with the objective of capturing the high ground west of the town. A fourth attacked from the south up the Gennep-Nijmegen highway, pushing aside two platoons at Plasmolen and moved on toward Mook, with the objective of seizing the Heumen lock bridge over the Maas-Waal Canal to choke off British vehicular traffic moving up from Eindhoven.

Single platoons fought uneven battles against ten to twenty times their number. The two platoons of 508th PIR troopers at Beek were forced to pull back to the hill at Berg-en-Dal, while the 505th PIR defenders were pushed back a half mile to the outskirts of Groesbeek and were overrun at Mook to the south, threatening the bridge at Heumen. On Hill 75.9, known as "Devil's Hill," two platoons of Company A and one platoon of Company G, 508th PIR, held out against heavy attacks by enemy paratroopers, though cut off from the main line of resistance.

Gavin had every rifle company in the division committed, and the division was stretched to the breaking point against over-whelming odds. Gavin, who was in Nijmegen to help with the river crossing by the 504th PIR later that day, reluctantly returned to his command post to be briefed on the current situation. Then, he left for the most critical point, Mook, because of the danger to the single bridge across the Maas-Waal Canal that was capable of bearing vehicular traffic. Ekman, who had arrived earlier, organized a counterattack that succeeded in pushing a reinforced battalion of German paratroopers out of the town in particularly savage house-to-house fighting.

General Gavin would later say that September 20, had been "a day unprecedented in the division's combat history."

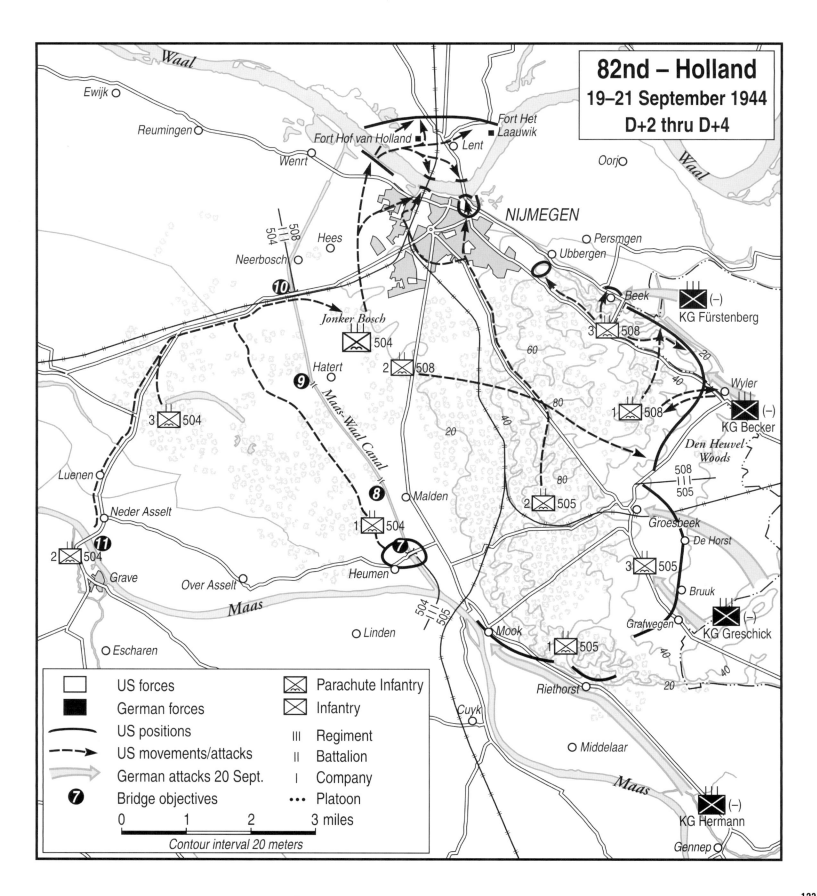

82nd – Holland
19–21 September 1944
D+2 thru D+4

Waal

Ewijk

Reumingen

Wenrt

Fort Het Laauwik

Fort Hof van Holland

Lent

Oorj

Waal

NIJMEGEN

508
504

Hees

Persmgen

Ubbergen

Neerbosch

10

Jonker Bosch

504

Beek

KG Fürstenberg

3 508

Hatert

2 508

60

Wyler

9

Maas-Waal Canal

1 508

20

40

KG Becker

3 504

Den Heuvel Woods

80

508
505

Luenen

8

1 504

Malden

40

80

2 505

Neder Asselt

11

Groesbeek

2 504

7

De Horst

Grave

Over Asselt

Heumen

3 505

Maas

Bruuk

Linden

504
505

Grafwegen

KG Greschick

Escharen

Mook

1 505

40

Riethorst

40

Cuyk

20

Middelaar

Maas

KG Hermann

Gennep

Legend

☐	US forces	⊠	Parachute Infantry
■	German forces	⊠	Infantry
⌒	US positions	III	Regiment
- - ➤	US movements/attacks	II	Battalion
➡	German attacks 20 Sept.	I	Company
❼	Bridge objectives	•••	Platoon

0   1   2   3 miles

Contour interval 20 meters

The 505th PIR Command Post in the woods west of Groesbeek, Holland. *Photograph courtesy of Jerome V. Huth*

Top right: A British Sherman tank is shown on the main highway through Mook during the fighting on September 20. The convent building in the background was turned into a German strongpoint. *U.S. Army photograph, courtesy of the 82nd Airborne Division War Memorial Museum*

Middle right: The main road through Mook shortly after the fighting ended on September 20. A British tank knocked out during the struggle can be seen on the left. *Photograph by William Jenks*

Bottom right: Colonel William E. Ekman, who personally organized the counterattack to evict the German forces from Mook, rides down the main road in his jeep shortly after the town was cleared of enemy troops on September 20, 1944. *Photograph by William Jenks*

Chapter 25

"I'VE NEVER SEEN A MORE GALLANT ACTION"

At around 2:30 p.m. on September 20, 1944, Companies E and F, 505th PIR, and tanks of the Grenadier Guards began the attack on Hunner Park, the traffic circle, and the Belvoir villa on the southern approaches of the great highway bridge in Nijmegen. Hunner Park was defended by around six hundred tough panzer grenadiers of the 9th SS Reconnaissance Battalion who were dug in, along with several 20mm antiaircraft guns. The Belvoir was defended by paratroopers of the Hermann Göring Training Regiment.

About 120 paratroopers with each of the two rifle companies poured out of houses and formed a skirmish line as they ran toward the enemy positions. The Germans opened up from well concealed, dug-in positions as Vandervoort's veteran paratroopers closed on them, firing their weapons as they charged. In brutal, close-range and hand-to-hand fighting, the paratroopers moved through the park, across the traffic circle, and toward the Belvoir.

As this was occurring, the 3rd Battalion, 504th PIR, began the epic crossing of the Waal River, from a position west of the huge power plant on the southern bank of the great river. The first wave was made up of Companies H and I; engineers from Company C, 307th Airborne Engineer Battalion, to shuttle the boats back across the river to carry more troopers across; and some 3rd Battalion headquarters troopers with Major Julian Cook, the battalion commander. As Cook's veteran paratroopers rowed the twenty-six flimsy boats, with plywood bottoms and canvas sides, toward the northern shore of the fast flowing river, Germans on the dike road a few hundred yards north of the shore opened up with machine guns, mortars, and small-arms fire. Long-range artillery began to find the range. From the right flank, 20mm antiaircraft fire rained down from the railroad bridge, and enemy troops in Nijmegen around the rail yard opened up from the right rear.

With shrapnel and bullets hitting the water, in what looked like rain drops, the troopers rowed frantically as some were being killed and wounded, helpless in their small boats. As the first boats touched down, troopers immediately began moving toward the dike road. Only thirteen of the twenty-six boats that started out made the far shore, and only eleven were able to make the trip back to pick up the rest of the 3rd Battalion, 504th PIR.

The troopers with Companies H and I advanced to the dike road and quickly killed or drove off the defenders. Then, some troopers chased the survivors across fields and orchards, while others attacked Fort Hof Van Holland and the northern end of the railroad bridge to the east.

Watching the entire crossing and assault from the power plant, and commenting on the incredible bravery shown by Tucker's paratroopers, British General Browning turned to the British XXX Corps Commander, General Brian Horrocks, and said, "I have never seen a more gallant action."

The aftermath of the terrible fighting in which Company F, 505th PIR, captured Hunner Park, September 20, 1944. *Photograph courtesy of the 82nd Airborne Division War Memorial Museum*

This 88mm antiaircraft gun, located on northwest side of the Keizer Lodewijkplein traffic circle in Nijmegen, did much damage to British armor. *Photograph courtesy of the Cornelius Ryan Collection, Alden Library, Ohio University*

Facing Page: The 504th PIR's objectives on September 20, 1944, are seen in this photograph: the northern ends of the railroad bridge (lower left) and the highway bridge (lower right) over the Waal River. Fort Hof Van Holland can be seen in the left center of the photo. The dike road from which much of the German direct fire emanated runs from the upper left of the photo to the south side of Fort Hof Van Holland and under the railroad and highway bridges. *Photograph by 541 Squadron, RAF, courtesy of Frits Janssen*

These beautiful attached two- and three-story houses near the highway bridge in Nijmegen were set on fire by the Germans to prevent infiltration by Vandervoort's paratroopers. *U.S. Army photograph, courtesy of the Cornelius Ryan Collection, Alden Library, Ohio University*

Other sections of Nijmegen were devastated by German artillery fire. *U.S. Army photograph, courtesy of the Cornelius Ryan Collection, Alden Library, Ohio University*

Chapter 26

"I'M PROUD TO MEET THE COMMANDER OF THE FINEST DIVISION IN THE WORLD TODAY"

As Germans were being pushed out of Beek, Wyler, and Mook, the Germans defending the two Nijmegen bridges were getting squeezed from both ends. The 2nd Battalion, 505th PIR, and British tanks overran the SS grenadiers in Hunner Park. Of the six hundred or so enemy in the park, only about sixty prisoners were taken, about sixty escaped, and the rest were killed. Company F suffered over sixty killed or wounded. Company E casualties were comparatively light in the attack on the traffic circle and Belvoir. Heavy German artillery fire immediately began to fall on the southern approach to the highway bridge as the last of the defenders were overwhelmed, so as to interdict any attempts to cross it.

The 504th PIR paid a terrible cost to cross the Waal River, but closed in on the two bridges. Reaching the north end of the railroad bridge, one platoon of Company C, 307th Airborne Engineer Battalion, began looking for German demolition charges attached to the bridge supports, while nineteen troopers with Company H, 504th PIR, took up positions on the bridge surface. Seeing that they were about to be cut off, several hundred Germans ran across the bridge attempting to escape. The nineteen troopers let them come about two thirds of the way and called for them to surrender. When a few raised their hands and ran forward, they were shot by their own people. The small band of paratroopers opened fire on the Germans as they came toward them. The next morning, the bodies of 267 Germans were counted on the bridge.

Meanwhile, another group of paratroopers from Company I, 504th PIR, led by Captain T. Moffatt Burriss captured the north end of the highway bridge after a firefight. A short time later, the troopers heard the sound of tanks approaching in the fading sunlight. They jumped in a ditch with Gammon grenades at the ready. When the tanks got close enough, the troopers discovered that they were British tanks of the Grenadier Guards. After a short celebration with the British, the paratroopers urged them to move up the road to Arnhem. The tanks edged down the road and were fired on by a German antitank gun. The tanks pulled back and the commander refused to advance, even after an offer by Burriss to take his troopers with them and knock out the gun together.

That night, the 504th RCT consolidated its bridgehead. It had lost forty-eight troopers killed or missing during the crossing and capture of the north ends of the two bridges.

The following morning, the Germans attacked the bridgehead with infantry supported by two Mark VI Tiger I tanks and a half-track. Company C's Private John Towle, the only bazooka gunner in the battalion with ammunition, moved forward of the company's positions about a hundred yards. He almost single-handedly stopped the attack by firing from behind a dike, then moving and firing from another position over the dike. He killed nine Germans setting up a machine gun. As he kneeled to fire at the half-track he was killed by mortar shrapnel. The enemy withdrew a short time later. Towle

would later be posthumously awarded the Congressional Medal of Honor for his courage.

Eyewitness accounts of the Waal River crossing by General Browning, General Adair, and General Horrocks made their way to General Sir Miles Dempsey, commander of the British Second Army, who visited Gavin at the 82nd Airborne Division Champion Command Post on September 23. As Dempsey entered, Gavin saluted and Dempsey returned the salute and extended his hand, saying, "I'm proud to meet the commanding general of the finest division in the world today."

The initial objective of the 3rd Battalion, 504th PIR, was the dike road that appears at the upper left of the photo. After seizing the dike, some of the troopers chased the survivors northeast to the trestle where the railroad crosses over the dike road. Meanwhile, other troopers moved east on the dike road and attacked Fort Hof Van Holland, then on to the north end of the railroad bridge. *Photograph by 541 Squadron, RAF, courtesy of Frits Jansse*

This German 75mm antitank gun was positioned between the railroad and highway bridges north of the Waal River to have a clear field of fire on any vehicles that crossed the bridges. The 3rd Battalion, 504th PIR, took out this antitank gun during its attack west to capture the highway bridge. *Photograph by 541 Squadron, RAF, courtesy of Frits Janssen*

This German was killed on the deck that ran beside the roadway on the highway bridge. *U.S. Army photograph, courtesy of the Cornelius Ryan Collection, Alden Library, Ohio University*

A dead German SS panzer grenadier lies on the highway bridge. A Very pistol, used to fire flares, lies beside him. *U.S. Army photograph, courtesy of the Cornelius Ryan Collection, Alden Library, Ohio University*

These concrete blocks on the bridge ramp were used by the Germans to block the north end of the highway bridge. The opening was covered by German antitank guns. *Photograph courtesy of the Cornelius Ryan Collection, Alden Library, Ohio University*

A British tank rolls across the highway bridge at Nijmegen and past the body of a German soldier killed defending it. *U.S. Army photograph, courtesy of the Cornelius Ryan Collection, Alden Library, Ohio University*

In this photograph, two German wooden flak towers can be seen above the concrete blocks. *Photograph courtesy of the Cornelius Ryan Collection, Alden Library, Ohio University*

British General Sir Miles Dempsey greets General Gavin with a handshake and the famous words, "I'm proud to meet the commanding general of the finest division in the world today." *Photograph courtesy of the Cornelius Ryan Collection, Alden Library, Ohio University*

Chapter 27

"I'M SURE GLAD YOU BASTARDS ARE HERE"

After the failure of the British Second Army to force a crossing of the Rhine River, the fighting in Holland settled into static warfare reminiscent of the First World War. The 82nd Airborne Division continued to hold the corridor north of the Maas River to the bridgehead north of the Waal River.

With ammunition running extremely low, the defenders on Devil's Hill held off the last of the German attacks on September 21 and were relieved on the night of September 24. At 4:30 a.m. on September 23, the 508th PIR attacked to clear the flatlands south of the Waal River and drove eastward to Erlekom, Hill 9.2, and Thorensche Molen.

By the late morning of the 23rd, the weather cleared in England sufficiently for the 325th GIR; Batteries D, E, and F, 80th Airborne Antiaircraft (Antitank) Battalion; division special troops (reconnaissance platoon, MP platoon); and Headquarters, 307th Airborne Engineer Battalion, to take off for Holland in 406 Waco gliders. Some of the gliders cut loose early, and others in the serials followed, landing in the corridor to the south in the 101st Airborne sector, including the glider that carried the commanding officer of the 325th GIR, Colonel Charles Billingslea. However, 348 gliders landed in the area of Landing Zone "O," near Over Asselt.

After landing and assembling, the 2nd Battalion, 325th GIR, moved to a hill west of the Kiekberg Woods and relieved the 1st Battalion, 505th PIR. When Lieutenant Edgar L. Cook, with Company E, 325th, approached one

of the 505th officers to coordinate the relief, the officer said to Cook, "I'm sure glad you bastards are here."

The 2nd Battalion, 401st GIR, took over the area to their left, from Knapheide to Horst to Heikant. This relieved the 505th PIR to move to Nijmegen to guard the two Waal River bridges against sabotage or demolition by Germans frogmen infiltrating down the Waal River at night.

On the morning of September 25, the Germans attacked the 2nd Battalion, 325th GIR, and after bitter fighting and a counterattack, the enemy was forced to withdraw. From September 27 to 30, the 2nd Battalion, 325th GIR, and the 2nd Battalion, 401st GIR, attacked to clear the Kiekberg Woods, but were only able to penetrate part of the way due to fierce enemy resistance and the dense undergrowth that made unit cohesion difficult.

On the 29th of September, the 505th PIR was relieved from guarding the Nijmegen bridges. That night after the 505th PIR was relieved, German frogmen used demolition charges to drop the center span of the railroad bridge into the Waal River and lightly damage the highway bridge.

On October 1 and 2, the Germans launched massive attacks supported by tanks and self-propelled guns at the entire perimeter of the division, managing to make some penetrations. The division's artillery and company-sized counterattacks pushed the Germans back to their start lines, inflicting heavy casualties on them.

The 325th GIR launched attacks south of Mook to clear the plains so that the British could build pontoon bridges across the Maas River to carry additional traffic. The battle seesawed back and forth until the glider troopers were able to capture the ground.

With both sides depleted and exhausted, the fighting died down on October 3. Night patrols by both sides, as well as artillery and mortar barrages, became the primary means of combat until the division was relieved by the Canadian Army on November 10. The division

A glider pilot and two 82nd Airborne glider troopers, prior to takeoff on September 23, 1944. *Photograph courtesy of the Silent Wings Museum*

Colonel Charles Billingslea replaced Colonel Harry Lewis as commanding officer of the 325th GIR when Lewis was sent to the United States after being diagnosed with terminal cancer. *U.S. Army photograph, courtesy of the Cornelius Ryan Collection, Alden Library, Ohio University*

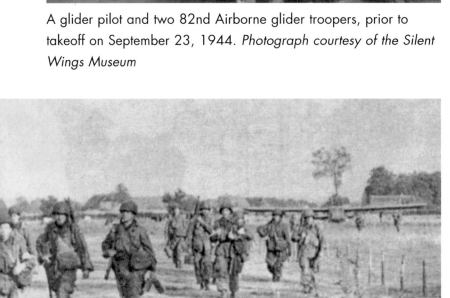

Troopers of the 325th GIR move to assemble after landing at Landing Zone "O," near Over Asselt, Holland, on September 23, 1944. *Photograph courtesy of the Cornelius Ryan Collection, Alden Library, Ohio University*

Two troopers advance across the open flat ground in Holland as a shell explodes nearby. *U.S. Army photograph, courtesy of the 82nd Airborne Division War Memorial Museum*

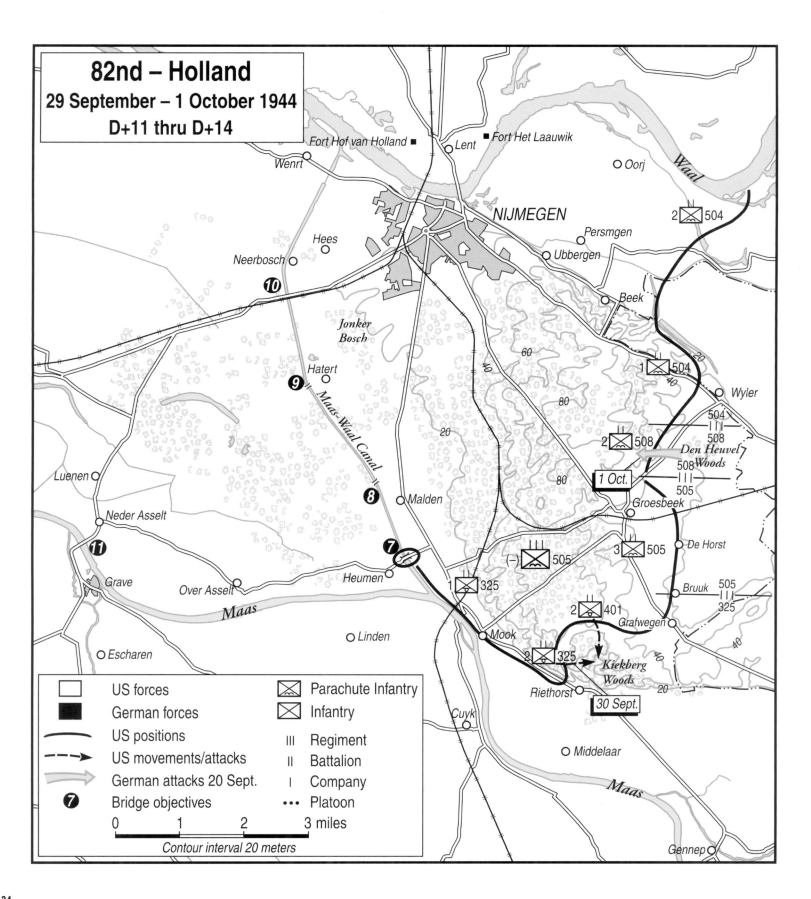

82nd – Holland
29 September – 1 October 1944
D+11 thru D+14

Fort Hof van Holland ■ Lent ■ Fort Het Laauwik

Wenrt

○ Oorj

Waal

NIJMEGEN

2 [⊠] 504

Hees ○

Persmgen ○

Neerbosch ○

○ Ubbergen

⑩

Beek ○

Jonker Bosch

60

Hatert ○

1 [⊠] 504

40

20

⑨

Maas-Waal Canal

○ Wyler

80

504 ||| 508

2 [⊠] 508

Den Heuvel Woods

Luenen ○

20

80

508 ||| 505

Neder Asselt ○

⑧

○ Malden

1 Oct.

Groesbeek ○

⑪

⑦

Heumen

(−) [⊠] 505

3 [⊠] 505

○ De Horst

Grave

Over Asselt ○

Maas

1 [⊠] 325

Bruuk 505 ||| 325 ○

2 [⊠] 401

Grafwegen ○

○ Linden

Mook ○

2 [⊠] 325

Kiekberg Woods

○ Escharen

Riethorst ○

30 Sept.

Cuyk ○

40

20

○ Middelaar

Legend

□	US forces	[⊠]	Parachute Infantry
■	German forces	[⊠]	Infantry
⌒	US positions	|||	Regiment
- -▶	US movements/attacks	||	Battalion
▶	German attacks 20 Sept.			Company
⑦	Bridge objectives	•••	Platoon

0   1   2   3 miles

Contour interval 20 meters

Maas

Gennep ○

Weldon Grissom, with Company H, 505th PIR, holds a German MP40 "burp gun," taken as a souvenir during the fighting in Holland.
Photograph courtesy of Weldon Grissom

An aerial photo of the Kiekberg Woods (bottom left) and Landing Zone "N" (bottom right and center). The 325th GIR fought from September 27 to October 1, 1944, to take this wooded area. The very dense undergrowth made contact between units even as small as squads almost impossible. The Germans were dug in, well camouflaged, and used mutually supporting fire to frustrate the glider troopers. *Photograph by 541 Squadron, RAF, courtesy of Frits Janssen*

General Dempsey, commander of the British Second Army, receives a briefing by General Gavin, September 28, 1944. *U.S. Army photograph courtesy of the Cornelius Ryan Collection, Alden Library, Ohio University*

The Nijmegen railroad bridge after German frogmen successfully dropped the center span into the Waal River. *Photograph courtesy of Jerome V. Huth*

The 75mm artillery of the 319th Glider Field Artillery, the 376th Parachute Field Artillery, and 456th Parachute Field Artillery Battalions was instrumental in stopping the massive German attacks of October 1 and 2, 1944. *Photograph courtesy of Jerome V. Huth*

A dead German, killed during the attacks of October 1 and 2. *U.S. Army photograph courtesy of the Cornelius Ryan Collection, Alden Library, Ohio University*

A German self-propelled gun, knocked out while attacking the 82nd Airborne Division perimeter, October 1–2. *U.S. Army photograph, courtesy of the Cornelius Ryan Collection, Alden Library, Ohio University*

An aerial photo of Middelaar, Holland, located south of Riethorst and north of the Maas River, on the Mook plains. The 325th GIR captured the ground in an all-day struggle on October 2, 1944, costing the regiment nine officers and 280 men killed, wounded, and missing. Note the many shell holes in the lower half of the photo, as well as the zigzag German trench lines crisscrossing the area. *Photograph by 541 Squadron, RAF, courtesy of Frits Janssen*

These French army barracks at Camp Sissone, France, near Rheims, were the home for much of the division from the last half of November until December 18, 1944. *Photograph courtesy of Thomas Kent*

Chapter 28

"LET'S GET THE SONS OF BITCHES!"

On December 16, 1944, the Germans launched a massive offensive in the Ardennes area of Belgium and Luxembourg. They achieved complete surprise and broke through the thinly held portion of the American line. The only strategic reserve for the U.S. Army in Europe was the 82nd and 101st Airborne Divisions, at encampments near Rheims, France, after over sixty days of fighting in Holland. On the night of the 17th, Gavin alerted his staff and the division for a movement to Belgium.

The next morning, the division was loaded into truck transports and driven to the small town of Werbomont, on the northern shoulder of the Bulge. The following morning, December 19, the 504th RCT moved northeast toward the Amblève River, the 505th RCT moved east toward the Salm River, the 508th RCT moved southeast to the Thier-du-Mont ridgeline and Vielsalm, and the 325th RCT moved south to the Fraiture area.

On the afternoon of December 20, the Companies B and C, 504th PIR, moved northeast of Rahier along a road that led to the tiny hamlet of Cheneux, which overlooked a bridge over the Amblève River. There, a bridgehead was held by a reinforced motorized flak battalion of the 1st SS Panzer Division's Kampfgruppe Peiper. The two parachute infantry companies were ordered to attack and wipe out that bridge-head. As the paratroopers emerged from woods on each side of the road about dusk, they were hit by massive machine gun fire from dug-in positions and 20mm antiaircraft fire from flak wagons, half-tracks, and wheeled reconnaissance vehicles.

Attacking in four waves, Tucker's veterans closed with the Germans as their skirmish lines were decimated. A young Private First Class Mike Holmstock crawled forward as he saw tracers zipping overhead. "About that time, I heard [Staff Sergeant William P.] "Knobby" Walsh up on the road, yelling for hand grenades. He said, 'Let's get the sons of bitches, they're killing us.'" Led by NCOs and platoon leaders, the two rifle companies engaged the Germans at close range and in hand-to-hand fighting as they overran their positions in front of the town. However, they suffered so many casualties that they were only able to hold a western end of the town.

During the predawn hours, Company G, 504th PIR, attacked and was forced to withdraw with heavy casualties as it ran into automatic weapons fire from three sides as it moved into the town. Later that morning, the Germans made a counterattack, and with the help of a barrage from the 376th Parachute Field Artillery, the 504th PIR inflicted terrible casualties on the fanatical SS troopers.

Troopers with the 1st Battalion, 504th PIR, move through Rahier on the way to Cheneux, December 20, 1944. *U.S. Army photograph, courtesy of the 82nd Airborne Division War Memorial Museum*

Tank destroyers attached to the 82nd Airborne Division move up in the fog toward Cheneux, December 20, 1944. *U.S. Army photograph, courtesy of the 82nd Airborne Division War Memorial Museum*

The view of this photograph is northeasterly toward the town of Cheneux. The road from Rahier runs from left to center. Companies B and C, 504th PIR, moved out of the woods on both sides of the road at left center and attacked across open ground toward the town. German half-tracks and flak wagons were positioned on the road beginning at the bend in the road. German machine guns and infantry were dug in on the ridge right side of the photo and in front of the town on the left side of the road. *U.S. Army photograph, courtesy of the 82nd Airborne Division War Memorial Museum*

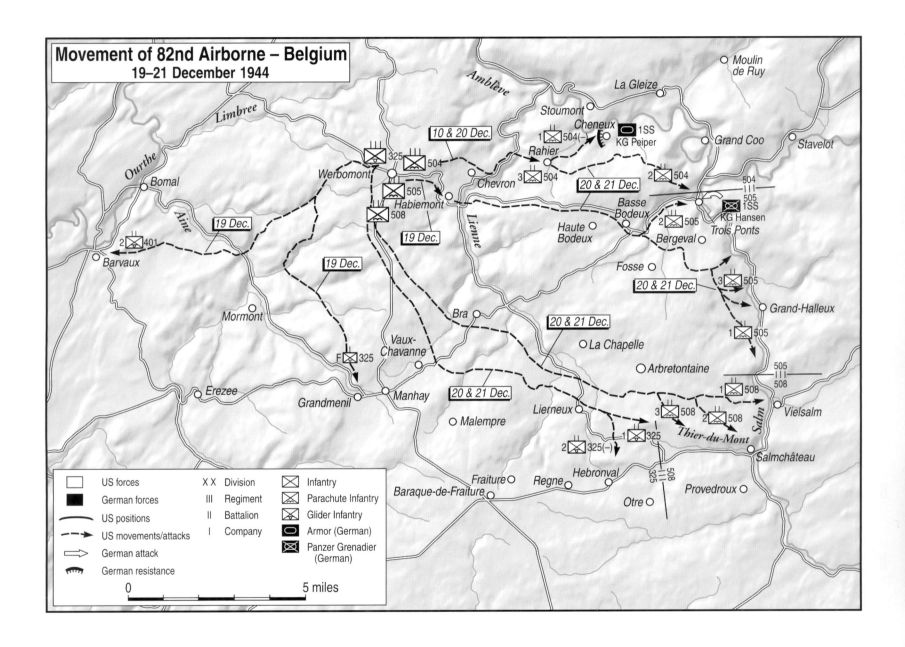

Movement of 82nd Airborne – Belgium
19–21 December 1944

Moulin de Ruy

Amblève

La Gleize

Stoumont

Cheneux

10 & 20 Dec.

Grand Coo

Stavelot

1 ☒ 504(−)

1SS
KG Peiper

Rahier

325

504

3 ☒ 504

2 ☒ 504

504
III
505

Werbomont

Chevron

20 & 21 Dec.

Basse Bodeux

1SS
KG Hansen

505

Habiemont

508

Lienne

Haute Bodeux

2 ☒ 505

Trois Ponts

Bomal

Aisne

19 Dec.

19 Dec.

Bergeval

2 ☒ 401

Fosse

3 ☒ 505

Barvaux

19 Dec.

Grand-Halleux

1 ☒ 505

Mormont

20 & 21 Dec.

Bra

La Chapelle

Vaux-Chavanne

Arbretontaine

505
III
508

F ☒ 325

Erezee

Grandmenil

Manhay

20 & 21 Dec.

Lierneux

Malempre

1 ☒ 508

Vielsalm

3 ☒ 508

2 ☒ 508

1 ☒ 325

Thier-du-Mont

Salm

Salmchâteau

2 ☒ 325(−)

325
III
508

Fraitureo

Regne

Hebronval

Provedroux

Baraque-de-Fraiture

Otre

☐ US forces	X X Division	☒ Infantry
■ German forces	III Regiment	☒ Parachute Infantry
⌒ US positions	II Battalion	☒ Glider Infantry
- -► US movements/attacks	I Company	⬤ Armor (German)
⇨ German attack		☒ Panzer Grenadier (German)
⌢ German resistance		

0   5 miles

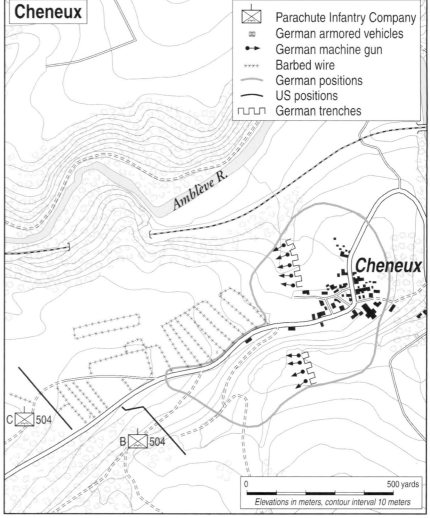

A 504th PIR trooper stands in front of a German half-track captured at Cheneux and painted with stars to identify it as a friendly vehicle to Allied fighter-bomber aircraft. *U.S. Army photograph, courtesy of the 82nd Airborne Division War Memorial Museum*

A destroyed German flak wagon sits in Cheneux after the attack by the 504th PIR. *U.S. Army photograph, courtesy of the 82nd Airborne Division War Memorial Museum*

Chapter 29

"I'M THE 82ND AIRBORNE, AND THIS IS AS FAR AS THE BASTARDS ARE GOING!"

As the fighting at Cheneux raged on the evening of December 20, the 1st SS Panzer Division moved west to force a crossing of the Salm River. The 505th PIR had reached the river's key crossing sites only hours earlier. The 2nd Battalion defended Trois Ponts, with Company E sent across the river to establish a bridgehead on the heights that overlooked the town on the eastern side. Company F was positioned in the town, while Company D defended a railroad crossing and foot-bridge south of the town.

Shortly after dawn on the 21st, Company E was hit by an attack by an overwhelming force of the 1st SS Panzer Grenadier Regiment, a battalion of heavy tank destroyers, and another of self-propelled armored 105mm artillery. Heavily outnumbered, Company E stopped a full-scale infantry attack supported by four or five tank destroyers, with enemy dead lying among the company's foxholes. With Company E dug in with its back to a steep bluff, the situation was critical. Vandervoort sent Company F across the river and it hit the German left flank just as another attack was being launched. Vandervoort was finally given permission to withdraw, and drove across the river and gave the order personally. The two companies conducted a fighting withdrawal as the Germans pressed to wipe them out. They successfully made it across the river and to the town, then stopped the Germans infantry as it crossed the river behind them.

That afternoon, a combined attack by the 1st and 3rd Battalions of the 504th PIR succeeded in capturing Cheneux and thus eliminating the Germans' bridgehead over the Amblève River, sealing the fate of Kampfgruppe Peiper.

South of Trois Ponts, Company I, 505th PIR, defended the next road bridge crossing at Rochelinval. Elements of the 1st SS made an attack at dusk on Company I, which repulsed the assault and blew the bridge as the first German armored vehicles reached it.

That night, another attack hit Company G at Petit and Grand-Halleux to the south. Again the attack was thrown back and the bridge blown.

At the southern end of the 82nd Airborne Division defense line on the Salm River, Company A, 508th PIR, defended the three bridges at Vielsalm and screened the withdrawal of the U.S. forces from St.-Vith on December 22 and 23.

On the open right flank of the division, the 2nd SS Panzer Division moved north up the road from Houffalize to Werbomont. The 325th GIR defended the southern flank on a line running from the Thier-du-Mont ridgeline to the village of Fraiture. Company F, 325th GIR, was sent to reinforce an ad hoc group of defenders at the key crossroads at Baraque-de-Fraiture to block the road to Werbomont. The highway that led west from Salmchâteau to Fraiture was used by the forces withdrawing from St.-Vith. As a tank destroyer moved along

Crews fire 81mm mortars in support of the 82nd Airborne Division's defense line. *U.S. Army photograph, courtesy of the 82nd Airborne Division War Memorial Museum*

the highway, the commander spotted a lone trooper from the 325th digging a foxhole for an outpost near the road. The commander stopped the vehicle and asked him if this was the frontline.

The trooper, Private First Class Vernon L. Haught, with Company F, 325th, looked up and said, "Are you looking for a safe place?"

The tank destroyer commander answered, "Yeah."

Haught replied, "Well buddy, just pull your vehicle behind me. I'm the 82nd Airborne, and this is as far as the bastards are going."

On the morning of December 23, elements of the 2nd SS Panzer Division hit the 2nd Battalion, 325th GIR, defenders at Fraiture and at Baraque-de-Fraiture. A strong counterattack by the 2nd Battalion threw back the enemy at Fraiture, inflicting heavy losses on the SS panzer grenadiers. However, Company F was surrounded at Baraque-de-Fraiture, and after several full-scale attacks, the crossroads was overrun. Most of Company F was killed or captured, with only about forty escaping.

The 2nd Battalion, 325th GIR, moves out from Werbomont in a heavy fog, December 20, 1944. *U.S. Army photograph courtesy of the National Archives*

Company I, 505th PIR, troopers dug in along the railroad embankment at Rochelinval, Belgium, fire across the Salm River at elements of the 1st SS Panzer Division. *Photographic still of U.S. Army combat film*

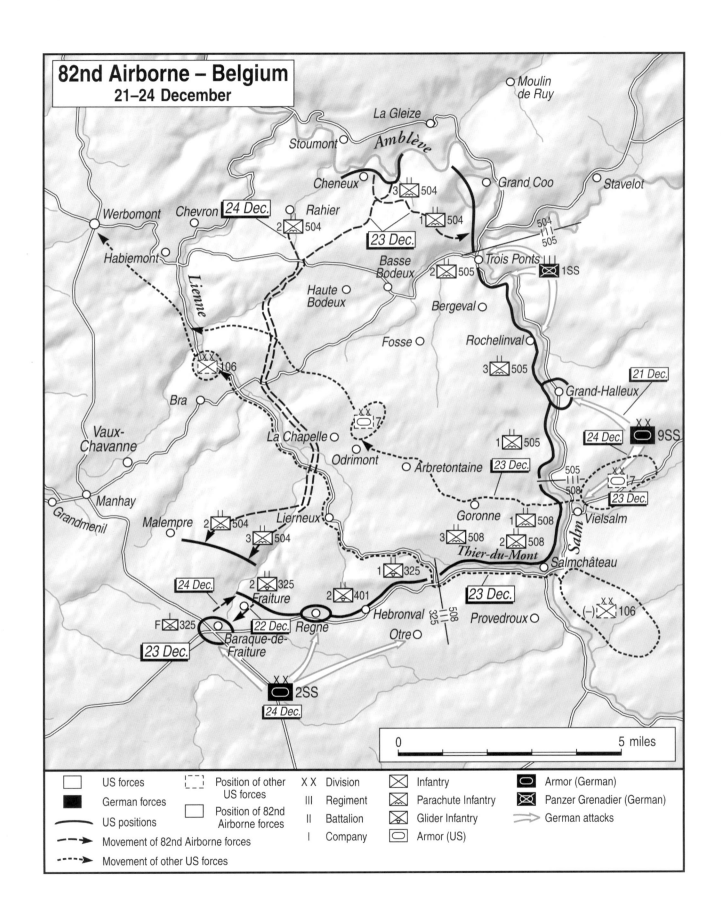

82nd Airborne – Belgium
21–24 December

Moulin de Ruy

La Gleize

Ambléve

Stoumont

Cheneux

3 [X] 504

Grand Coo

Stavelot

Werbomont

Chevron

24 Dec.

Rahier

2 [X] 504

1 [X] 504

23 Dec.

504
505

Habiemont

Basse Bodeux

Trois Ponts

2 [X] 505

1SS

Lienne

Haute Bodeux

Bergeval

Rochelinval

Fosse

3 [X] 505

21 Dec.

Bra

XX 106

Grand-Halleux

Vaux-Chavanne

XX 7

La Chapelle

Odrimont

Arbretontaine

1 [X] 505

24 Dec.

9SS

23 Dec.

505
508

XX 7

Manhay

Grandmenil

Malempre

2 [X] 504

3 [X] 504

Lierneux

Goronne

1 [X] 508

3 [X] 508

2 [X] 508

23 Dec.

Vielsalm

Thier-du-Mont

Salmchâteau

Salm

24 Dec.

2 [X] 325

Fraiture

1 [X] 325

2 [X] 401

Hebronval

508
325

23 Dec.

Provedroux

(–) XX 106

F [X] 325

22 Dec.

Regne

Otre

23 Dec.

Baraque-de-Fraiture

XX 2SS

24 Dec.

| 0 | | 5 miles |

US forces		Position of other US forces		X X	Division		[X]	Infantry		Armor (German)
German forces		Position of 82nd Airborne forces		III	Regiment		[X]	Parachute Infantry		Panzer Grenadier (German)
US positions				II	Battalion		[X]	Glider Infantry		German attacks
Movement of 82nd Airborne forces				I	Company		Armor (US)		
Movement of other US forces									

A bazooka team with Company C, 325th GIR, mans a roadblock near Bosson on December 23, 1944, as German armor threatens to turn the right flank and encircle the division. Very tough defense by the 325th GIR delayed the 2nd SS Panzer Division until the fall of the Baraque-de-Fraiture crossroads on December 23, 1944. *U.S. Army photograph, courtesy of the National Archives*

The crew of a 57mm antitank gun of the 80th Airborne Antiaircraft (Antitank) Battalion defend one of the roads along the division's perimeter in Belgium. *U.S. Army photograph, courtesy of the 82nd Airborne Division War Memorial Museum*

One of the houses overrun by the 2nd SS Panzer Division at the crossroads at Baraque-de-Fraiture. *Photograph courtesy of John F. Gatens*

Staff Sergeant James Martin, Company F, 325th GIR, is photographed as he returns from outpost duty near Ordimont, Belgium. A two-piece paratrooper version of the bazooka can be seen hanging by the strap from Martin's left arm. This is perhaps the most famous photograph of the division during WWII. *U.S. Army photograph, courtesy of the National Archives*

"SORT OUT THE BATTLEFIELD AND TIDY UP THE LINES"

With the way open from Baraque-de-Fraiture, the division was in grave danger of being encircled when the 2nd SS Panzer Division pushed on to Werbomont. With every regiment in the division committed, Gavin shifted his forces to meet this threat. He ordered the 2nd Battalion, 504th PIR, to be moved to the vicinity of Lansival.

Additionally, the 2nd SS overran the town of Regne in the 325th GIR sector in an attempt to overwhelm Colonel Billingslea's glider troopers. Company B and a company of tanks counterattacked and retook the town. A short time later, the Company B troopers ambushed and captured the regimental adjutant of one of the 2nd SS regiments, along with a copy of the division's plans for the next several days. This information proved invaluable in the coming days.

Meanwhile, at Vielsalm, the last of the forces withdrawn from St.-Vith crossed the bridges late on December 23. Following on their heels, elements of the 9th SS Panzer Division attacked to capture the bridges before they could be blown. Company A, 508th PIR, fought tenaciously to drive the enemy back from the eastern side of the river in a series of gallant counterattacks while engineers tried unsuccessfully to fix the demolition charge on the one remaining intact bridge. Finally, Company A troopers placed a box of C-2 plastic explosive on the bridge and fired a bazooka round into it, demolishing the last bridge.

On the morning of December 24, the division was facing elements of three of Germany's most powerful SS panzer divisions, as well as a volksturm division. It was in real danger of being surrounded, because the 3rd Armored Division was unable to secure the area on the division's right flank.

Meanwhile, British Field Marshall Montgomery, who had been given the command of all forces on the northern shoulder of the bulge, arrived that morning at the XVIII Airborne Corps Headquarters Command Post at Werbomont. He told Ridgway that the 82nd Airborne Division "could now withdraw with honor to itself and its units." Montgomery ordered Ridgway to withdraw the division, repeating much of the same that he had said four days earlier at General Courtney Hodges' command post, saying it was time to "sort out the battlefield and tidy up the lines. After all, gentlemen, you can't win a big victory without a tidy show."

For the first time in its history, the division would retreat in the face of the enemy. It was a bitter pill for most of the officers and men of the division, who felt that they could hold their positions indefinitely against any enemy force. That night the division conducted a textbook withdrawal to new positions dug in along a series of hills running southwest from Trois Ponts to just east of Manhay.

Christmas Day would be clear enough for the troopers to watch Allied fighter-bombers strafe and bomb enemy vehicles and troop concentrations in the distance. Some of the lucky men in the division actually ate a turkey dinner with the trimmings, but many didn't see one at all.

That night, the 9th SS Panzer Division hit the 2nd Battalion, 508th PIR, but was forced to withdraw after some savage close-quarter fighting with the paratroopers. The following night, the 3rd Battalion, 508th PIR, was hit at Erria and temporarily overrun. With help from the 2nd Battalion, a strong counterattack recaptured the town in house-to-house fighting. Enemy attacks died out as the division's troopers prepared for the inevitable counteroffensive to retake the ground that they had given up.

From left to right, Privates Charles Badeaux, Theodore Sohoski, and John Bogdan, all with the 80th Airborne Antiaircraft (Antitank) Battalion, worship at a makeshift altar on Christmas Day, 1944. *U.S. Army photograph, courtesy of the 82nd Airborne Division War Memorial Museum*

Troopers with the 505th PIR line up with their mess kits for a turkey dinner, served from buckets and crates. *Photograph by Daniel B. McIlvoy, courtesy of Ann McIlvoy Zaya*

Troopers happily consume doughnuts served out of ammunition crates. *U.S. Army photograph, courtesy of the 82nd Airborne Division War Memorial Museum*

Paratroopers with Company H, 504th PIR, ambushed a German patrol of SS grenadiers near Bra, Belgium, killing several and capturing one. They are shown taking the prisoner back to the main line of resistance, December 25, 1944. *U.S. Army photograph, courtesy of the 82nd Airborne Division War Memorial Museum*

The 82nd Airborne Division Band plays Christmas songs for some of the troopers brought off the line, December 25, 1944. *U.S. Army photograph, courtesy of the 82nd Airborne Division War Memorial Museum*

This photograph of Erria was taken on January 7, 1945. It shows the total devastation resulting from the fighting between the 508th PIR and elements of the 9th SS Panzer Division. *U.S. Army*

General Gavin, carrying his M1 rifle, walks alone toward the command post of the 3rd Battalion, 508th PIR, to get a firsthand look at the situation during the attack by the 9th SS Panzer Division at Erria, Belgium, December 27, 1944. *U.S. Army photograph, courtesy of the National Archives*

Troopers with Company H, 505th PIR, practice with a bazooka in preparation for the offensive on January 3, 1945. *Photograph courtesy of Weldon Grissom*

Gavin visits the 3rd Battalion, 508th PIR, command post during the fighting at Erria, December 27, 1944. *U.S. Army photograph, courtesy of the 82nd Airborne Division War Memorial Museum*

These troopers in the rear area live in the relative luxury of dugouts near Vaux-Chavanne, Belgium, December 29, 1944. *U.S. Army photograph, courtesy of the 82nd Airborne Division War Memorial Museum*

Three gun positions of the 254th Field Artillery Battalion, camouflaged with netting, December 30, 1944. *U.S. Army photograph courtesy of the 82nd Airborne Division War Memorial Museum*

The 254th Field Artillery Battalion, which had been a part of the U.S. 106th Infantry Division before its destruction, was attached to the 82nd Airborne Division and served the division well with its powerful 155mm howitzers. *U.S. Army photograph, courtesy of the 82nd Airborne Division War Memorial Museum*

The 105mm howitzers of Battery A, 320th Glider Field Artillery Battalion, helped to turn back the German attacks from December 25 to 27. *Photograph by Paul Speakman, courtesy of the 82nd Airborne Division War Memorial Museum*

The division reconnaissance platoon used jeeps like this, mounted with a .50-caliber machine gun. *U.S. Army photograph, courtesy of the 82nd Airborne Division War Memorial Museum*

A religious service is held for troopers prior to the counteroffensive of January 3, 1945. *U.S. Army photograph, courtesy of the 82nd Airborne Division War Memorial Museum*

Two troopers man an outpost in the deepening snows prior to January 3, 1945. *U.S. Army photograph, courtesy of the 82nd Airborne Division War Memorial Museum*

"WELL COLONEL, THE OLD GUYS GOT IT TODAY"

On January 3, 1945, the 82nd Airborne Division launched attacks in one to two feet of snow to capture the ground it had relinquished only ten days earlier. The 325th GIR attacked the high ground at Heid-de-Heirlot and advanced under heavy enemy fire to just north of the villages of Amcomont and Ordimont. The 505th PIR in the center attacked and captured the hamlets of Noirfontaine, Reharmont, and Fosse, and in the process destroyed two enemy battalions. However, the losses were appalling, as the Germans dug in on the high ground and firing from stone buildings exacted a terrible price before the troopers closed with them. Two-thirds of the men and every officer in Company I were killed or wounded in their attack on Fosse.

That afternoon, a wounded Sergeant Bill Tucker, with Company I, 505th PIR, was evacuated to the aid station at Basse-Bodeux, where the 505th command post was located. "[Lieutenant] Colonel Krause, who had become the regimental executive officer, paced up and down. I said to him, 'Well Colonel, the old guys got it today.' Colonel Krause stopped. He gazed at me and beyond me. There were tears in his eyes."

To their left, the newly attached 517th PIR attacked Trois Ponts and the high ground to the southwest. The 551st Parachute Infantry Battalion, which was attached to the 517th PIR, attacked on the right side of the regiment and ran into tough resistance as it approached the high ground at Herispeche. A flanking move forced the Germans to withdraw. The 517th PIR moved through Trois Ponts against limited opposition before

fire from the high ground to the southwest at Mont-de-Fosse stopped it cold. It made a night attack to capture the ground and was on its phase line by sunrise the following morning. The freezing weather and snow made for a miserable night for the troopers in the rifle companies.

Before dawn on January 4, the 2nd Battalion, 325th GIR, skirted the village of Heirlot and hit it from the rear, surprising and overwhelming the Germans defending the town. The 2nd Battalion, 401st GIR, captured Amcomont and Ordimont by that afternoon.

The 505th PIR advanced south against light opposition, having wiped out the two enemy battalions facing it the previous day. Only the 2nd Battalion encountered any significant resistance, as the Germans fought to deny the only road and supply route south to the 505th PIR. The 517th PIR spent most of the day consolidating its positions after capturing St.-Jacques, Bergeval, and Monte-de-Fosse before dawn that morning.

On January 5, the division pressed the attack, with the 1st Battalion, 325th GIR, capturing the high ground between Arbrefontaine and La Falise to the southwest. The 2nd Battalion, 505th PIR, moved into Arbrefontaine against only a rear guard, while the 1st and 3rd Battalions advanced a thousand yards against almost no opposition. The 551st PIB attacked and captured Dairomont without any casualties, while the 517th PIR repulsed a strong enemy attack at Bergeval. The 504th PIR was now committed on the left flank of the 505th PIR, with the 3rd Battalion taking the high ground overlooking Grand- and Petit-Halleux. The division rested and consolidated its gains on January 6.

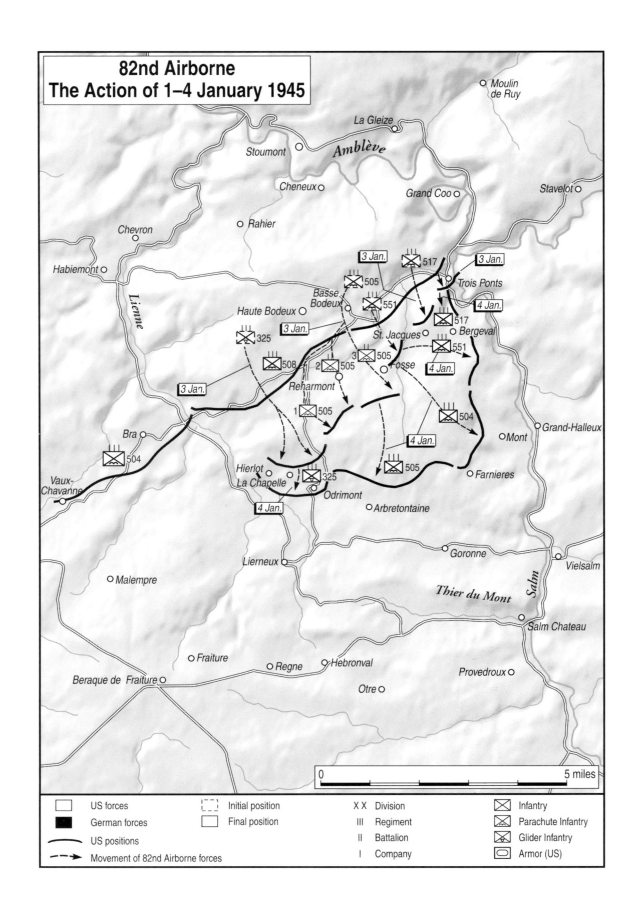

82nd Airborne
The Action of 1–4 January 1945

Moulin de Ruy

La Gleize

Amblève

Stoumont

Cheneux

Grand Coo

Stavelot

Chevron

Rahier

Habiemont

Lienne

3 Jan. ⊠ 517

3 Jan.

⊠ 505

Trois Ponts

3 Jan.

Basse Bodeux

⊠ 551

4 Jan.

Haute Bodeux

⊠ 517

3 Jan.

⊠ 325

St. Jacques

Bergeval

⊠ 551

⊠ 508

3 ⊠ 505

Fosse

4 Jan.

2 ⊠ 505

3 Jan.

Reharmont

1 ⊠ 505

⊠ 504

Grand-Halleux

4 Jan.

Mont

Bra

⊠ 505

Farnieres

⊠ 504

Hierlot

⊠ 325

La Chapelle

Vaux-Chavanne

Odrimont

4 Jan.

Arbretontaine

Goronne

Vielsalm

Lierneux

Salm

Malempre

Thier du Mont

Salm Chateau

Fraiture

Regne

Hebronval

Provedroux

Beraque de Fraiture

Otre

0   5 miles

US forces	Initial position	X X Division	⊠ Infantry
German forces	Final position	III Regiment	⊠ Parachute Infantry
US positions		II Battalion	⊠ Glider Infantry
Movement of 82nd Airborne forces		I Company	⬭ Armor (US)

153

Troopers with the 325th GIR pile their overcoats, sleeping bags, and other non-essential gear along the trail before making the attack on Heid-de-Heirlot, Belgium, on January 3, 1945. *U.S. Army photograph, courtesy of the 82nd Airborne Division War Memorial Museum*

The 2nd Battalion, 325th GIR, lines up prisoners captured during the attack on the high ground at Heid-de-Heirlot before marching them to a POW holding area. *U.S. Army photograph, courtesy of the 82nd Airborne Division War Memorial Museum*

Well built and concealed bunkers such as these had to be cleared during the costly attacks of January 3, 1945. *U.S. Army photograph, courtesy of the 82nd Airborne Division War Memorial Museum*

This German prisoner captured at Fosse, Belgium, during the bloody attack by Companies H and I, 505th PIR, on January 3, 1945, appears to be age fifteen or sixteen. *U.S. Army photograph, courtesy of the 82nd Airborne Division War Memorial Museum*

German prisoners are processed at Basse-Bodeux, January 3, 1945. *U.S. Army photograph, courtesy of the National Archives*

German POWs are interrogated by the division G-2 intelligence section in front of the command post at Werbomont, Belgium. *U.S. Army photograph, courtesy of the 82nd Airborne Division War Memorial Museum*

An enemy prisoner (center) smiles as he marches with his hands up into captivity. He knew that the Americans treated POWs well. He could expect a warm place to stay and hot food, unlike the troopers who had to continue in the attack. *Photograph by Daniel B. McIlvoy, courtesy of Mrs. Ann McIlvoy Zaya*

The division's organic artillery, the 75mm pack howitzers, moved forward to support the rifle companies during the attacks of January 3–6, thanks to herculean efforts by the artillerymen. *U.S. Army photograph, courtesy of the 82nd Airborne Division War Memorial Museum*

The 82nd Signal Company performed heroically, often under direct enemy fire, to run field telephone lines to the forward units as the division attacked through the deep snow and freezing cold. *U.S. Army photograph, courtesy of the 82nd Airborne Division War Memorial Museum*

Troopers with the 505th PIR advance with a tank destroyer down the road from Basse-Bodeux to Arbrefontaine, January 4, 1945. *Photograph by Daniel B. McIlvoy, courtesy of Mrs. Ann McIlvoy Zaya*

The 307th Airborne Engineer Battalion uses an armored bulldozer to clear the single road supplying the division during the attacks of January 3–5. *U.S. Army photograph courtesy of the National Archives*

The same bulldozer, only moments later, clears an enemy self-propelled gun on the road near Heirlot, Belgium, January 4, 1945. *U.S. Army photograph, courtesy of the 82nd Airborne Division War Memorial Museum*

Paratroopers of the 1st Battalion, 505th PIR, advance behind a tank of the 636th Tank Destroyer Battalion, January 4, 1945. The tank on the left side of the photograph is out of action with a missing right tread. *U.S. Army photograph, courtesy of the 82nd Airborne Division War Memorial Museum*

These troopers with the 505th PIR advance along this wooded trail with a tank, looking for possible enemy positions on each side of the trail. *Photograph by Daniel B. McIlvoy, courtesy of Mrs. Ann McIlvoy Zaya*

Colonel William E. Ekman, the commander of the 505th PIR. *Photograph by Robert M. Piper, courtesy of Robert M. Piper*

General Gavin was always up front with the attacking elements during the day, staying in touch with his command post via radio. Gavin would return to the CP at night to receive a briefing on the overall situation and get a few hours of sleep. *U.S. Army photograph, courtesy of the 82nd Airborne Division War Memorial Museum*

Engineers with Company A, 307th Airborne Engineer Battalion, have one of the German crew of this 75mm antitank gun disable a booby trap in the breech of the gun, near Ordimont, Belgium. *U.S. Army photograph, courtesy of the 82nd Airborne Division War Memorial Museum*

Lieutenant Stanley Weinberg, with Company B, 505th, with newly acquired German snow cape and Sturmgewehr 44, also known as an MP44, January 5, 1945, near Arbrefontaine, Belgium. This weapon was the world's first assault rifle, firing shorter and lighter 7.92mm ammunition than the standard German rifle round, utilizing a thirty-round magazine and a switch to allow either semiautomatic or fully automatic firing. *Photograph courtesy of Ms. Ann Weinberg*

These troopers with Company B, 505th PIR, have about as much comfort as could be expected. A pup tent is pitched, several troopers are gathered around a small fire (left), and their wet overcoats and other clothing hang from the limbs of the tree to dry, Arbrefontaine, Belgium, January 5, 1944. *Photograph by Stanley Weinberg, courtesy of Ms. Ann Weinberg*

Chapter 32

"SIR, THEY'RE ALL DEAD"

The division resumed the attack on January 7, 1945. Almost every rifle company had been bled white by the fighting over the previous four days on ground that they had occupied only a couple of weeks before.

On the right, the 1st Battalion, 325th GIR, seized the small villages of Menil, Brux, and Gernechamps, and the 2nd Battalion, 325th GIR, passed through their line to attack and capture the high ground at Thier-de-Preux. They repulsed a heavy German counterattack later that day.

The 508th PIR had been brought forward from division reserve the previous day. With Company G leading, it attacked and captured the Thier-du-Mont ridgeline in a short but brutal fight at close quarters. Company G overran a battery of 88mm antiaircraft guns at the edge of the wooded slope that had used direct fire against them as they advanced across eight hundred yards of open ground below. To their left, the 505th PIR attacked southeast to capture Goronne, but lost one of its most beloved commanders when Lieutenant Colonel Benjamin Vandervoort was wounded in an eye by mortar shrapnel during the attack on the high ground overlooking the town.

The hard-luck 551st PIB, now down to half strength, made a gallant attack across open ground against a numerically superior German force dug in on the bluff above to seize the town of Rochelinval. Lieutenant Dick Durkee, with Company A, led his troopers forward up the slope toward the German machine guns that were raking his small force. By the time Durkee had reached the outskirts of the town, he only had one man with him. "I saw one man fifty yards down the draw from my position. I recognized him as my runner; his name, Private [Pat] Casanova. I yelled to him to get those riflemen up here in a hurry so it would be possible to attack the town. His answer, I'll never forget, 'Sir, they're all dead.'"

The 551st PIB's attack finally captured Rochelinval after an assault that lasted all day. The battalion virtually ceased to exist as an effective fighting unit, and was later disbanded, with the survivors being sent to rifle companies in the division as replacements.

The following day, the 504th PIR cleaned out Petit-Halleux and put patrols across the Salm River into Grand-Halleux. The 505th PIR moved up and occupied the high ground overlooking the river north of Rencheux. On January 9, the 2nd Battalion, 505th PIR moved into Rencheux across the Salm River from Vielsalm.

The next day, the division consolidated its positions and was relieved on the night of January 10–11 by the U.S. 75th Infantry Division. The division was trucked to rest areas a few miles to the north at Theux, Pepinster, Chevron, and Remouchamps. After a few days of rest, the division began training and integrating replacements for the next action that would come all too soon.

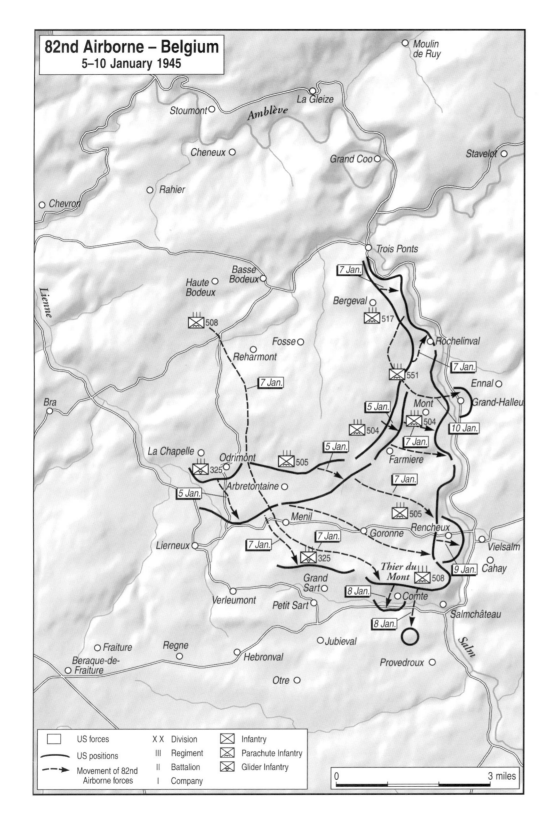

82nd Airborne – Belgium
5–10 January 1945

Moulin de Ruy
Stoumont
La Gleize
Amblève
Cheneux
Grand Coo
Stavelot
Rahier
Chevron
Trois Ponts
7 Jan.
Basse Bodeux
Haute Bodeux
Bergeval
508
517
Fosse
Reharmont
7 Jan.
Rochelinval
7 Jan.
551
Ennal
Grand-Halleu
Bra
5 Jan.
Mont
504
504
10 Jan.
La Chapelle
325
Odrimont
505
5 Jan.
7 Jan.
Farmiere
Arbretontaine
5 Jan.
7 Jan.
Menil
Lierneux
7 Jan.
7 Jan.
Goronne
505
Rencheux
Vielsalm
325
Thier du Mont
508
9 Jan.
Cahay
Grand Sart
8 Jan.
Comte
Salmchâteau
Verleumont
Petit Sart
8 Jan.
Fraiture
Regne
Jubieval
Provedroux
Beraque-de-Fraiture
Hebronval
Otre
Lienne
Salm

US forces — US positions — Movement of 82nd Airborne forces
X X Division — III Regiment — II Battalion — I Company
Infantry — Parachute Infantry — Glider Infantry

0   3 miles

Two troopers on outpost duty with the 325th GIR near Ordimont, Belgium, keep a watch for enemy activity to their front, January 6, 1945. *U.S. Army photograph, courtesy of the 82nd Airborne Division War Memorial Museum*

Captain Joseph Kenny, one of the 508th PIR chaplains, holds a mass on January 6, 1945, for troopers of the 3rd Battalion, who will lead the attack on the Thier-du-Mont ridgeline the following day. *U.S. Army photograph, courtesy of the National Archives*

Paratroopers with the 508th PIR move into a Belgian village on January 6, 1945, in preparation for the attack the following day. *U.S. Army photograph, courtesy of the National Archives*

This partially demolished barn serves as an outpost for a light machine gun crew of the 508th PIR, January 6, 1945. *U.S. Army photograph, courtesy of the National Archives*

Two troopers with the 1st Battalion, 505th PIR, track down German soldiers near Goronne, Belgium, January 7, 1945. *U.S. Army photograph, courtesy of the 82nd Airborne Division War Memorial Museum*

A dead German lies in front of a wrecked American jeep near Arbrefontaine, Belgium, January 7, 1945. The jeep had been captured and used by the Germans until it was machine gunned by troopers of the 82nd Airborne Division, wrecking it and killing the driver. *U.S. Army photograph, courtesy of the National Archives*

Artillerymen prepare to fire a 75mm pack howitzer in support of attacks by the division. *U.S. Army photograph, courtesy of the National Archives*

A trooper leads a column of POWs to the rear. *Photograph courtesy of the 82nd Airborne Division War Memorial Museum*

A trooper with the 325th GIR stands next to an SS trooper captured wearing a pair of jump boots. Enemy soldiers, especially the SS, caught wearing jump boots were dealt with harshly. *U.S. Army photograph, courtesy of the National Archives*

Paratroopers with the 505th PIR inspect a German Mark VI Tiger II tank knocked out near Goronne, Belgium, January 7, 1945, killing the entire crew. Belgian girls (left) smile and look admiringly at the troopers as they pass. *U.S. Army photograph, courtesy of the National Archives*

The 2nd Battalion, 325th GIR on the way to a rest area at Pepinster, Belgium, after being relieved by the U.S. 75th Infantry Division, January 10, 1945. *U.S. Army photograph, courtesy of the National Archives*

A column of troopers march down an ice-covered road in the Belgian forest during the attacks toward the Salm River. *Photograph courtesy of the 82nd Airborne Division War Memorial Museum*

A trooper snaps a photo of his buddy during good times at the rest area, January 15, 1945. *U.S. Army photograph, courtesy of the National Archives*

Colonel Reuben H. Tucker, commander of the 504th PIR (left), and Major Julian Cook, commander of the 3rd Battalion, 504th PIR (second from left), receive the Distinguished Service Cross from Lieutenant General Lewis Brereton, commanding general of the First Allied Airborne Army, at Remouchamps, Belgium, January 20, 1945. They displayed extraordinary heroism in leading the assault crossing of the Waal River in Holland. *U.S. Army photograph, courtesy of the National Archives*

Lieutenant John L. Foley receives the Distinguished Service Cross at Remouchamps, Belgium, January 20, 1945, for extraordinary heroism leading the great stand by Company A, 508th PIR, on Devil's Hill in Holland. *U.S. Army photograph, courtesy of the National Archives*

Members of the division reconnaissance platoon test German Panzerfausts and a U.S. bazooka on the frontal armor of a Mark VI Tiger II tank at La Gleize, Belgium. The Panzerfausts made the deepest penetration, only four inches of the seven inches of the frontal armor. *U.S. Army photograph, courtesy of the National Archives*

Captain Wesley D. Harris receives the Distinguished Service Cross for extraordinary gallantry in leading Company C, 307th Airborne Engineer Battalion, during the assault crossing of the Waal River in Holland, in a ceremony at Remouchamps, Belgium, January 20, 1945. *U.S. Army photograph, courtesy of the National Archives*

Chapter 33

"SURRENDER, HELL!"

At 6:00 a.m. on January 28, the 82nd Airborne Division and the 1st Infantry Division spearheaded the U.S. First Army's attack northeastward from St.-Vith to pierce the Siegfried Line. The attacks were made in knee-deep snow and bitterly cold conditions.

Foregoing the usual artillery barrage, the 325th GIR, attacking on the left, and the 504th PIR, on the right, caught the Germans eating breakfast in their billets and overran them before they could put up much resistance. The 325th GIR moved east through Meyerode and then took Wereth at 5:00 a.m. the following morning after a sharp fight. After moving twelve hours through the deep snow on January 28, the Company H, 504th PIR, ran into and destroyed an entire German battalion outside of Herresbach, Belgium, then held the town against repeated German counterattacks that night.

The following morning, the 505th PIR moved through the 325th GIR and pushed two thousand yards northeast to capture the high ground southwest of Honsfeld, Belgium. The 508th PIR moved through the 504th PIR that morning, and the 1st Battalion, 508th PIR, attacked and captured Holzheim, Belgium, taking a number of prisoners. As the battalion was consolidating its positions in and around the town, a German patrol entered the town, apparently unaware that it was in the hands of the 508th PIR, because everyone on both sides was wearing white snow capes with hoods. Seeing a group of German prisoners lined up, the officer leading the patrol and his men jumped two guards at one end of the line and began rearming the prisoners, with the intention of retaking the town.

Hearing a commotion, the first sergeant of Company C, 508th PIR, Leonard Funk, walked over to one of the guards, Private Merrel Arthur, and asked him what was going on. Not sure what was happening, Arthur saw three men in snow capes approach, and one of them pointed his weapon at them. "The German officer was waving his Schmeisser at Funk and jabbering and wanted us to drop our weapons. Funk looked a little bewildered at what was going on until the captured patrol man told us they were captured and now we are to become their prisoners, 'He wants us to surrender.'

"Funk started mumbling to himself softly like, 'Surrender, hell,' as in not knowing what to do, sort of pondering it.

"He was standing there with his Tommy gun slung arms, and the German was standing there waving his Schmeisser in Funk's belly. In a flash, that gun was in the German's belly and he ripped off a burst. The German started to sink slowly down. When he was on his knees, he tried to raise his gun at Funk, but didn't have the strength to pull the trigger."

Funk then began firing at the rearmed Germans, killing twenty-one and wounding a number of others before the enemy group surrendered once more. Funk would later be awarded the Congressional Medal of Honor for his actions.

Over the next three days, the regiments continued to advance through the thick forests and deep snow, taking turns leading the advance until they came to the open ground on the Belgian-German border across from the fortifications of the German Siegfried Line.

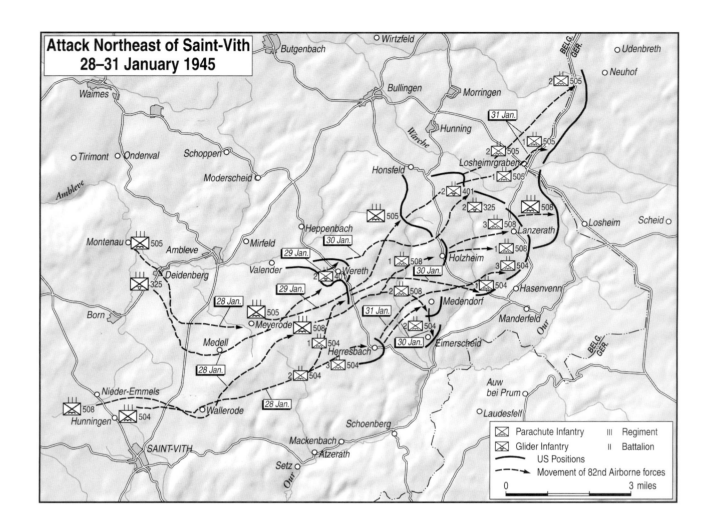

Attack Northeast of Saint-Vith
28–31 January 1945

Butgenbach ○ Wirtzfeld
Udenbreth ○
Neuhof ○
Waimes
2 ⊠ 505
Bullingen
Morringen
31 Jan.
Hunning
Warche
1 ⊠ 505
Tirimont ○ Ondenval ○
Schoppen ○
2 ⊠ 505
Moderscheid ○
Honsfeld
Losheimrgraben ○
1 ⊠ 505
Ambleve
2 ⊠ 401
505 ⊠
2 ⊠ 325
⊠ 508
Heppenbach ○
Losheim ○ Scheid ○
30 Jan.
3 ⊠ 508
Lanzerath
Montenau ○ ⊠ 505
Mirfeld ○
Ambleve
29 Jan.
1 ⊠ 508
⊠ 325
Valender
Holzheim
1 ⊠ 508
Deidenberg
Wereth
3 ⊠ 504
Born
28 Jan.
2 ⊠ 401
30 Jan.
1 ⊠ 504
Hasenvenn
29 Jan.
2 ⊠ 508
Medell
⊠ 505
Medendorf
Manderfeld
Meyerode
⊠ 508
31 Jan.
Our
1 ⊠ 504
2 ⊠ 504
BELG.
GER.
28 Jan.
Herresbach
Eimerscheid
30 Jan.
3 ⊠ 504
Nieder-Emmels ○
2 ⊠ 504
Auw
bei Prum ○
⊠ 508
⊠ 504
Wallerode ○
28 Jan.
Laudesfelf ○
Hunningen
Schoenberg ○

	Parachute Infantry	III	Regiment
SAINT-VITH	Glider Infantry	II	Battalion
	US Positions		
Mackenbach ○	Movement of 82nd Airborne forces		
Atzerath			

Setz ○
Our
0 _____ 3 miles

Company A, 325th GIR, deploy for an attack on a German roadblock as they move through snow almost hip deep, January 28, 1945. *U.S. Army photograph, courtesy of the National Archives*

Troopers with the 325th GIR pull a sled that holds their crew-served weapons along a trail broken by those ahead, January 28, 1945. *U.S. Army photograph, courtesy of the National Archives*

Company B, 325th GIR, moves toward Wereth, Belgium, January 28, 1945. *U.S. Army photograph, courtesy of the National Archives*

Troopers with Company E, 325th GIR, and Company F, 504th PIR, maintain contact as the two regiments attack east, January 28, 1945. *U.S. Army photograph, courtesy of the National Archives*

A trooper stands next to an imposing 88mm antitank gun overrun during the attack toward the Siegfried Line. *U.S. Army photograph, courtesy of the 82nd Airborne Division War Memorial Museum*

Troopers with Company G, 504th PIR, advance through deep snow along a firebreak with a Sherman tank from the attached 740th Tank Battalion near Herresbach, Belgium, January 28, 1945. *U.S. Army photograph, courtesy of the National Archives*

Paratroopers with the 504th PIR move along a firebreak toward Herresbach, Belgium, January 28, 1945. *U.S. Army photograph, courtesy of the National Archives*

Troopers with the 504th PIR follow the trail broken in the snow by the first man, during the attack toward Herresbach, Belgium, January 28, 1945. *U.S. Army photograph, courtesy of the National Archives*

These troopers gather around a Sherman tank before entering the field of small pine trees up ahead, near Herresbach, Belgium, January 28, 1945. *U.S. Army photograph, courtesy of the National Archives*

Troopers dressed in snow capes, and carrying their weapons and other gear, follow the trial left by the tank that has moved ahead on the road, near Herresbach, Belgium, January 28, 1945. Note that two of the troopers are carrying two M1 rifles. *U.S. Army photograph, courtesy of the National Archives*

This Weasel uses the snowplow on the front to clear deep snow from a trail near Herresbach, Belgium, January 28, 1945. *U.S. Army photograph, courtesy of the National Archives*

The division's military police guard the remnants of the German battalion destroyed at Herresbach the previous day, January 29, 1945. *U.S. Army photograph, courtesy of the National Archives*

German POWs line up to be processed by the division's military police and intelligence personnel. *U.S. Army photograph, courtesy of the 82nd Airborne Division War Memorial Museum*

Medics' jeeps have difficulty following the 1st Battalion, 505th PIR, as it moves toward Weneck, Belgium, January 29, 1945. *U.S. Army photograph, courtesy of the National Archives*

Medics used Weasels to evacuate the wounded, as well the cases of frostbite and trench foot. *U.S. Army photograph, courtesy of the National Archives*

As a jeep pulls into Amel, Belgium, paratroopers with the 505th PIR rest after the attack to capture the town, January 29, 1945. *U.S. Army photograph, courtesy of the National Archives*

Troopers with the 1st Battalion, 505th PIR, take a few minutes to read *The Stars and Stripes* newspaper in the woods outside Weneck, Belgium, shortly after the town was taken, January 29, 1945. *U.S. Army photograph, courtesy of the National Archives*

Jeeps and trailers of Service Company, 505th PIR, follow the regiment through deep snow, January 29, 1945. *U.S. Army photograph, courtesy of the 82nd Airborne Division War Memorial Museum*

The 1st Battalion, 508th PIR, moves into Holzheim, Belgium, January 29, 1945. *U.S. Army photograph, courtesy of the National Archives*

These two German POWs look shocked and demoralized after an attack. *Photograph courtesy of the 82nd Airborne Division War Memorial Museum*

German dead piled near a building in Holzheim after its capture by the 1st Battalion, 508th PIR, January 29, 1945. *Photograph courtesy of the 82nd Airborne Division War Memorial Museum*

First Sergeant Leonard A. Funk, Company C, 508th PIR, received every medal for valor awarded by the United States Army during World War II. He received the Congressional Medal of Honor for his heroic actions at Holzheim, Belgium, January 29, 1945. *U.S. Army photograph, courtesy of the 82nd Airborne Division War Memorial Museum*

The division command post at a farmhouse in eastern Belgium. *U.S. Army photograph, courtesy of the 82nd Airborne Division War Memorial Museum*

This trooper with Battery A, 320th Glider Field Artillery Battalion, has made his temporary home luxurious with his shelter half and a small wood-burning stove. *Photograph courtesy of the 82nd Airborne Division War Memorial Museum*

Troopers ride a tank into Diedenberg, Belgium. *U.S. Army photograph, courtesy of the 82nd Airborne Division War Memorial Museum*

Chapter 34

"THE CLOSEST TO HELL ONE COULD GET WITHOUT ENTERING THE GATES"

The 325th Glider Infantry Regiment attacked the formidable defenses of the Siegfried Line at 4:30 a.m. on February 2, 1945. The 1st Battalion attacked on the right, with the objective of the fortified town of Neuhof, while the 2nd Battalion, 401st GIR, attacked on the left to capture Udenbreth, a short distance to the north. In front of them in the darkness lay extensive minefields, barbed wire entanglements, dragon's teeth antitank obstacles, with the Germans waiting in concrete pill-boxes, interconnecting trenches, fortified houses, and at the edge of the forest beyond.

Braving intense German machine gun fire, the troopers, along with engineers from Company A, 307th Airborne Engineer Battalion, worked their way behind a few of the pillboxes and blew the doors with demolition charges, causing the Germans inside to surrender. Some then worked their way into the two villages, while others assaulted the pillboxes on both sides. Later that day, the glider troopers fought off a heavy counterattack supported by armor. It was a tough fight and the casualties were high, but the 325th GIR pried open the Siegfried Line.

To the right of this attack, the 504th PIR captured the Hertesrott Heights to the south, encountering well concealed enemy pillboxes and log-topped bunkers in the thick forest. Using Panzerfausts, Tucker's troopers blew open the doors or fired through the slits, usually forcing the surviving enemy to surrender. To the right of the

504th PIR, the 505th PIR attacked against light opposition, advancing up to four thousand yards.

On February 3, the Germans mounted several desperate counter-attacks to capture the ground lost the previous day. All were repulsed, with the enemy suffering heavy casualties.

From February 4 to 6, the division was relieved in place by the U.S. 99th Infantry Division. That same day, the 505th RCT was trucked north to the Hürtgen Forest, arriving at the town of Vossenack. On February 8, the rest of the division was trucked to the Hürtgen Forest. That day, the 505th RCT jumped off and advanced to the town of Kommerscheidt against almost no opposition. The route took them through the Kall River Valley, the scene of terrible fighting the previous fall. Sergeant Chris Christensen, upon witnessing the result of the carnage, would say, "What I had witnessed in the Hürtgen would leave a lasting impression. This place must have been the closest to hell one could get without entering the gates."

The following day, the division attacked through the forest toward the Roer River. The 508th PIR made a night attack at 2:00 a.m. on February 10, to capture Hill 400, which had changed hands numerous times in extremely bitter fighting the previous fall. Later that day, the division finished taking the ground up to the Roer River.

Between February 19 and 22, the division was relieved and trucked to its base camps in France. Replacements were received, passes for the troopers issued, training continued, reviews conducted, and decorations for valor awarded.

On April 2, the division was sent to Germany by train to defend the western side of the Rhine River near Cologne against a breakout attempt by German forces trapped in the Ruhr pocket. The division arrived on April 3 and 4 and began taking over positions of the U.S. 88th Infantry Division along the Rhine.

Top right: The dragon's teeth antitank obstacles and fortified houses that were part of the Siegfried Line. *U.S. Army photograph, courtesy of the 82nd Airborne Division War Memorial Museum*

Middle right: The troopers of the 82nd Airborne Division and tanks of the attached 740th Tank Battalion advance across open ground toward the Siegfried Line. *U.S. Army photograph, courtesy of the 82nd Airborne Division War Memorial Museum*

Bottom right: Troopers follow this tank as a precaution against landmines. The troopers of the division trained with the tankers of the 740th Tank Battalion during the time they spent in rest areas from January 11 to 26, 1945. *U.S. Army photograph, courtesy of the 82nd Airborne Division War Memorial Museum*

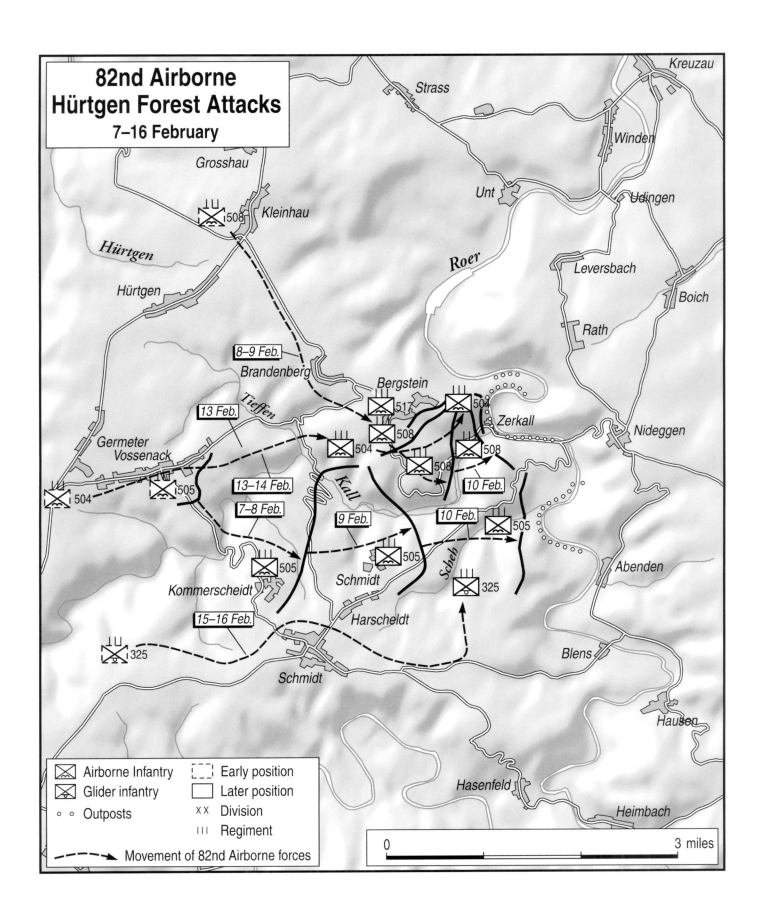

82nd Airborne
Hürtgen Forest Attacks
7–16 February

Kreuzau

Strass

Winden

Grosshau

Unt

Udingen

Kleinhau

Leversbach

Roer

Boich

Hürtgen

Hürtgen

Rath

8–9 Feb.

Brandenberg

Bergstein

517

504

Zerkall

13 Feb.

Tieffen

508

Nideggen

508

Germeter

504

504

Vossenack

508

508

13–14 Feb.

Kall

10 Feb.

504

505

7–8 Feb.

9 Feb.

10 Feb.

505

505

Schmidt

Scheb

Abenden

Kommerscheidt

325

15–16 Feb.

Harscheldt

Blens

325

Schmidt

Hausen

Hasenfeld

Heimbach

⊠ Airborne Infantry	⊡ Early position	
⊠ Glider infantry	☐ Later position	
∘ ∘ Outposts	x x Division	
	⊦⊦⊦ Regiment	
⤏ Movement of 82nd Airborne forces		

0   3 miles

This wreckage of American vehicles along the road through the Kall River valley in the Hürtgen Forest had been there since the previous fall. *Photograph by Robert M. Piper, courtesy of Robert M. Piper*

A signal corps cameraman crouching on a German pillbox is filming U.S. artillery shelling the town Zerkall, Germany, February 10, 1945. *U.S. Army photograph, courtesy of the National Archives*

Bodies of members of the 112th Infantry Regiment, 28th Infantry Division, killed the previous fall during fighting in the Hürtgen Forest. *Photograph by Robert M. Piper, courtesy of Robert M. Piper*

The 2nd Battalion, 325th GIR, moves through the devastated town of Schmidt, Germany, in the Hürtgen Forest area, February 17, 1945. *U.S. Army photograph courtesy of the National Archives*

Gavin awards Sergeant Lyle K. Kumler, Company H, 508th PIR, the Distinguished Service Cross on March 19, 1945, for his actions in leading the attack to recapture Beek, Holland. *U.S. Army photograph, courtesy of the National Archives*

On March 19, 1945, General Gavin pins the Distinguished Service Cross on the chest of First Sergeant Leonard A. Funk, Company C, 508th PIR, for his actions in leading the attack to clear the landing zone in Holland for incoming gliders. *U.S. Army photograph, courtesy of the National Archives*

Sergeant Charles E. Nau, Company B, 504th PIR, is awarded the Distinguished Service Cross by General Gavin on March 19, 1945, for his actions during the capture of Bridge Number 7 at Heumen, Holland. The trooper to the left of Gavin is Sergeant William P. Walsh, Company B, 504th PIR, who was awarded the Distinguished Service Cross for his actions during the attack at Cheneux, Belgium. *U.S. Army photograph, courtesy of the 82nd Airborne Division War Memorial Museum*

Troopers with Company B, 504th PIR, take a break during the train ride to Cologne, Germany area, April 1945. *Photograph courtesy of Bill Bonning*

Chapter 35

"REFUGEES FROM THE LAW OF AVERAGES"

On April 3, 1945, the division took over the sector along the Rhine River from Worringen, eight miles north of Cologne, extending south through Cologne, to Grau-Rheindorf, thirteen miles south of Cologne. The division set up positions in houses, factories, and commercial buildings along the waterfront, as well as listening posts along the river.

A plan to draw German forces away from the fighting east of the Rhine in the Ruhr pocket was initiated on April 6, when Company A, 504th PIR, crossed the Rhine River by boat at 2:30 a.m. to seize the town of Hitdorf on the eastern side. The landing was relatively uneventful, and Company A soon occupied the town. However, beginning later that morning, a German regiment of the 3rd Fallschirmjäger (Parachute) Division made a number of company-sized attacks supported by tanks on the individual platoons holding each side of the town. That afternoon the Germans overran two platoons and pushed into the center of town. Company A withdrew to the beach and formed a horseshoe-shaped perimeter. At 1:30 a.m. the following morning, Company I, 504th PIR, crossed the river, moved into the town, fought its way to the church that was used as the Company A command post, and evacuated the wounded to the Company A perimeter.

The two companies then evacuated by boat to the western side of the river. They had killed an estimated three hundred fifty and captured eighty enemy soldiers.

The remainder of the division's stay along the west side of the Rhine consisted primarily of patrolling across the river. After U.S. forces captured the area across the river, the division performed occupation duties in the areas west of the Rhine from April 16 to 25.

On April 26, the division was ordered to move by rail to northern Germany and execute an assault crossing of the Elbe River, then drive eastward to meet the Soviet forces to prevent them from moving into Denmark. The 505th PIR made the crossing shortly before 1:00 a.m. on the morning of April 30, catching the Germans by surprise. Enemy resistance was quickly overcome, and large numbers of prisoners were taken.

A pontoon bridge was constructed, and the division crossed and attacked through the 505th PIR on May 1. Elements of the 325th GIR reached the town of Ludwigslust on May 2. That afternoon, General Gavin established a command post in the town, and by the end of the night had met with and accepted the surrender of the German 21st Army Group, some 144,000 officers and men. Over the next several days, the division disarmed and processed these POWs. Contact was made with the Soviet Army, and lines of demarcation were agreed upon.

On May 5, the concentration camp at Wöbbelin, north of Ludwigslust, was discovered. Many of the troopers of the division visited the camp to bear witness to the atrocities of the Third Reich. The townspeople of Ludwigslust and a group of selected German Army officers were required to attend a funeral on May 7, 1945, for the victims, who were buried in the town square and those of a couple of nearby towns, Hagenow and Schwerin.

In the early morning hours of May 7, the unconditional surrender of all German forces was announced. Staff Sergeant Ross Carter, with Company C, 504th, was one of the very lucky men who served in a rifle company in the 82nd Airborne Division from North Africa to Germany. "My friends call me a refugee from the law of averages. My regiment still exists as a name, but the regiment in which I trained, fought, and almost died, now lies buried in obscure army cemeteries in ten countries."

This trooper reads a sign near the great cathedral in Cologne, warning "sightseers" to the front line areas that they draw artillery fire on the troopers. *U.S. Army photograph, courtesy of the 82nd Airborne Division War Memorial Museum*

The 82nd Airborne Division prepares to board trains at Düren, Germany, for the trip north to Bleckede, Germany, April 26, 1945. *U.S. Army photograph, courtesy of the National Archives*

Troopers wait in line to board their box car at Düren, Germany, April 26, 1945. *U.S. Army photograph, courtesy of the National Archives*

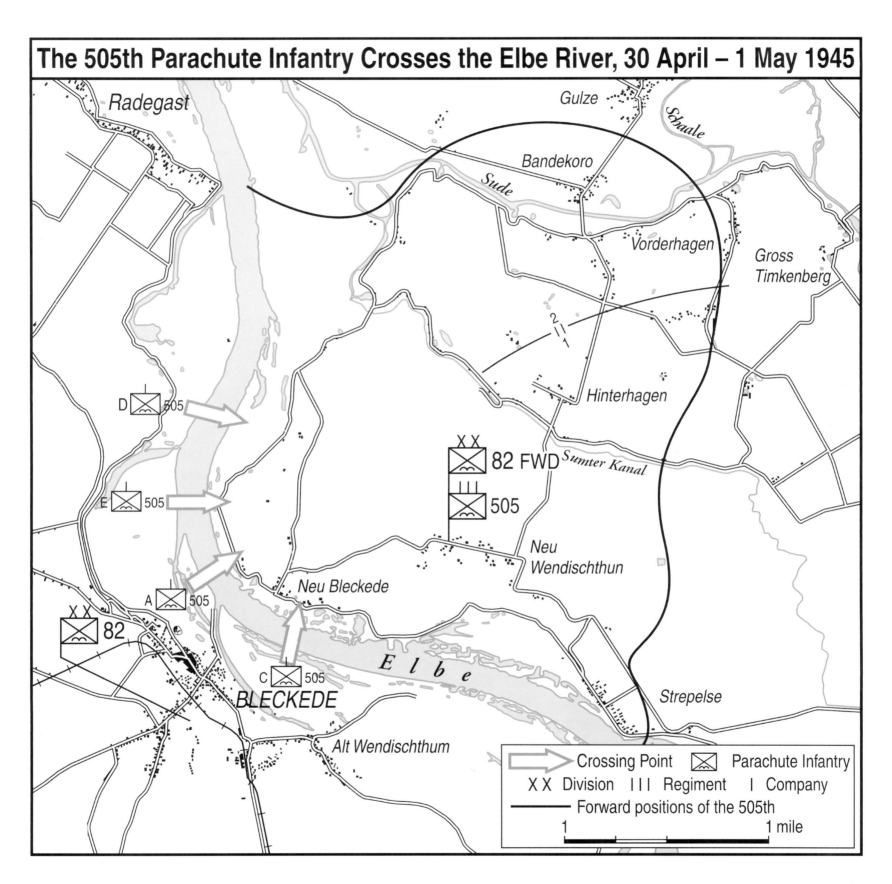

The 505th Parachute Infantry Crosses the Elbe River, 30 April – 1 May 1945

Radegast

Gulze

Schaale

Bandekoro

Sude

Vorderhagen

Gross Timkenberg

D ⊠ 505

E ⊠ 505

Hinterhagen

⊠⊠ 82 FWD

Sumter Kanal

⊠ 505

Neu Wendischthun

A ⊠ 505

⊠⊠ 82

Neu Bleckede

C ⊠ 505

BLECKEDE

Elbe

Strepelse

Alt Wendischthun

⟹ Crossing Point   ⊠ Parachute Infantry

X X Division   I I I Regiment   I Company

—— Forward positions of the 505th

1   1 mile

Members of the 3rd Battalion, 505th PIR, cross the Elbe River in Buffalos, April 30, 1945. *U.S. Army photograph, courtesy of the 82nd Airborne Division War Memorial Museum*

Some 505th PIR troopers rest against the dike, while others dig in, after crossing the Elbe River in amphibious vehicles, April 30, 1945. *U.S. Army photograph, courtesy of the National Archives*

Engineers of the 307th Airborne Engineer Battalion disarm one of the magnetically activated sea mines planted by the Germans along the road to Ludwigslust. *U.S. Army photograph, courtesy of the 82nd Airborne Division War Memorial Museum*

Some 144,000 German soldiers of the 21st Army Group march west into captivity after the commanding general surrendered unconditionally to the 82nd Airborne Division on May 2, 1945. These POWs are being held in a field while awaiting processing. *U.S. Army photograph, courtesy of the 82nd Airborne Division War Memorial Museum*

The citizens of Ludwigslust gather for the funeral service and burial of the victims of the Wöbbelin concentration camp, May 7, 1945. *U.S. Army photograph, courtesy of the 82nd Airborne Division War Memorial Museum*

Chapter 36

"YOU WONDER WHAT HAPPENS TO A MAGNIFICENT DIVISION OF BRAVE MEN AFTER THE WAR"

The division spent the last three weeks of May screening and guarding German POWs. Some of the men and officers with the highest number of points were sent home in May.

On June 1, 1945, the division was relieved and sent by train to Camp Chicago near Laon, France, arriving on June 5. A division review was held on June 9, and General Gavin announced that the division had been selected for occupation duty in Berlin. A second group of high-point men was sent home a few days later.

From June 12 to 15, the division moved again, to Epinal, France, where ceremonies was held on June 21 and 22 for a large group of high-point men departing for the United States. The division soon began receiving replacements from the deactivated 17th Airborne Division.

The division was loaded on trains at the end of July and arrived in Berlin between August 1 and 8. There were several clashes with gangs of unruly Soviet troops, in which about twenty of them were killed during the first month the division spent in Berlin. The Soviets learned to watch their behavior around the 82nd Airborne Division troopers.

Each regiment formed an honor guard to greet visiting dignitaries and high-ranking military officers. When General Patton reviewed the honor guard at a ceremony at Tempelhof Airport, he said, "In all of my years in the army and of all of the honor guards I've ever seen, the 82nd Berlin Honor Guard is the best."

In early October, the division received news that it would be disbanded. But, the division's public affairs officer, Lieutenant Colonel Barney Oldfield, who had been a newspaperman and press agent, mounted a news blitz in every U.S. newspaper with a circulation over ten thousand. The publicity of the impending disbanding of the division caused a groundswell of letter writing in the United States to the Secretary of War, who reversed the decision.

On December 29, 1945, the division left Europe on the *Queen Mary* for New York City. The division was selected over all of the other divisions in the military to lead the great 1946 New York City Victory Parade. The division arrived in New York on January 3, 1946. It spent the next week practicing close-order drills and marching. On January 12, the division marched up Fifth Avenue in the great tickertape parade, covered by the newsreel cameras. After the parade, many left for their homes and civilian life.

Martha Gellhorn, well-known war correspondent and at the time married to Ernest Hemingway, covered the 82nd Airborne Division during the Holland campaign for *Collier's* magazine. She wrote an article entitled "Rough and Tumble," in which she commented:

You are always happy [being] with fine combat troops, because in a way no people are as intensely alive as

A division review is held June 9, 1945, at Camp Chicago, near Laon, France. *U.S. Army photograph, courtesy of the National Archives*

they are. You do not notice the rain too much, or the ugly soaked flat land, or the sadness of the yellowing trees that are rotting limply from summer into the nakedness of winter. You do not think too much about what war costs, because you are too busy being alive for the day—too busy laughing and listening and looking. And you forget about the crude wooden crosses that mark where just such boys lie in Sicily and Italy and France and now Holland. You forget about the hospital in Nijmegen where devoted, weary men work in operating rooms that never cease to be appalling, no matter how many such operating rooms you have seen. You forget, too, that the boys who last it out intact and whole have nevertheless given up these years which were intended to be young and happy.

The years are gone. But, thinking it over afterward, you wonder what happens to a magnificent division of brave men after the war. And you wonder who is going to thank them, and will it be enough?

General Gavin salutes as the division passes in review at Camp Chicago, June 9, 1945. *U.S. Army photograph, courtesy of the National Archives*

Gavin, standing on a jeep (center right), announces that the division will be sent to Berlin for occupation duty, June 9, 1945. *U.S. Army photograph, courtesy of the National Archives*

The division arrived in Berlin to find much of the city in ruins. *U.S. Army photograph, courtesy of the 82nd Airborne Division War Memorial Museum*

Private First Class Gilbert E. "Ed" Dodd, Company C, 504th PIR, cooks his meal on his Coleman stove during the trip to Berlin. *Photograph courtesy of Ed Dodd*

Private First Class Ed Dodd, Company C, 504th PIR, stands on the rubble of a Berlin apartment building. *Photograph courtesy of Ed Dodd*

The Berlin Honor Guard awaits the arrival of General Patton at Tempelhof Airport, Berlin. *Photograph courtesy of Roy Kouski*

This apartment building in Berlin housed Company K, 325th GIR, formerly Company F, 401st GIR. *Photograph courtesy of Roy Kouski*

General George S. Patton Jr. (left) and General James M. Gavin (right) review the 82nd Airborne Division honor guard at Tempelhof Airport. *U.S. Army photograph, courtesy of the 82nd Airborne Division War Memorial Museum*

The Berlin Honor Guard marches under the Brandenburg Gate in Berlin. *U.S. Army photograph, courtesy of the 82nd Airborne Division War Memorial Museum*

General Gavin stands on the reviewing stand with Soviet commanders, including Marshall Georgi Zhukov (with baton in his left hand), at Tempelhof Airport. *U.S. Army photograph, courtesy of the National Archives*

A single officer and a single enlisted man were selected to represent the entire 82nd Airborne Division, at a ceremony on October 19, 1945, to receive the Netherlands government's Military Order of William, the Orange Lanyard of the Royal Netherlands Army. Lieutenant James Megellas, Company H, 504th PIR (center), was selected over all others in the division as the representative of the division's officers. *U.S. Army photograph, courtesy of the 82nd Airborne Division War Memorial Museum*

The *Queen Mary*, carrying the 82 Airborne Division, arrives in New York Harbor, January 3, 1946. *U.S. Army photograph, courtesy of the 82nd Airborne Division War Memorial Museum*

General Gavin sets the pace as the division begins its march up Fifth Avenue during the New York City victory parade, January 12, 1946. *U.S. Army photograph, courtesy of the 82nd Airborne Division War Memorial Museum*

The division passes under the arch at Washington Square. *U.S. Army photograph, courtesy of the National Archives*

The troopers of the 82nd Airborne Division march proudly up Fifth Avenue as people crowd the windows and balconies of buildings to watch. *U.S. Army photograph, courtesy of the National Archives*

Major General James M. Gavin salutes as he leads his proud division past the reviewing stand at the New York Public Library building. *U.S. Army photograph, courtesy of the 82nd Airborne Division War Memorial Museum*

The division passes the reviewing stand. *U.S. Army photograph, courtesy of the National Archives*

"Eyes left," as the units of the division march past the reviewing stand. *U.S. Army photograph, courtesy of the National Archives*

Heavy self-propelled artillery follows the division past the reviewing stand as the honor guard stands on both sides of the street at the reviewing stand. *U.S. Army photograph, courtesy of the National Archives*

Index